FAITH PASSAGES AND PATTERNS

By Thomas A. Droege

Edited by Allan Hart Jahsmann

Fortress Press, Philadelphia

LEAD Books

LEAD Books are prepared under the direction of the Division for Parish Services, the Lutheran Church in America.

Designed by Terry O'Brien.

Fifth printing 1990

Library of Congress Cataloging in Publication Data

Droege, Thomas A. (Thomas Arthur), 1931–
    Faith passages and patterns.

    (Lead books)
    1. Faith. 2. Trust in God. 3. Developmental
psychology. I. Jahsmann, Allan Hart. II. Title.
III. Series.
BT771.2.D75   1983   234'.2   82-48544
ISBN 0-8006-1602-2

Printed in the United States of America   1-1602

CONTENTS

FOREWORD

Faith development research and writings are currently flourishing, and Christians have good reason to be interested in these studies. As Dr. Droege reminds his readers in the last chapter of this book, the nurturing of faith is what the church's educational mission is all about. Church leaders, teachers, and parents are involved in the business of nurturing faith.

But what can theories of faith development in general tell us about the nurturing of *Christian* faith in particular? The author, a Christian theologian and teacher, acknowledges that Christian faith is fundamentally a gift, the workings of the Spirit of God. Nevertheless, he reminds us, God operates in and through nature and history. So we can expect a pattern in the way faith develops, and we can observe the conditions that seem to be necessary for growth in faith.

The author, a long-time student of Erik Erikson's human development theories and a recent fellow at the Emory University Center for Faith Development in Atlanta, Georgia, was asked to prepare a solid but simple (or simple but solid) summary of how persons grow in faith from infancy through adult stages. That was a big assignment in itself.

To make the book directly relevant to the teaching task of the church and the ministry of its leaders and teachers, the author also relates the findings of generic faith studies to *Christian* faith, its natural stages of growth and its nurture. By doing so he made the book a rare and valuable synthesis of theological and psychological insights.

Brief reflection activities precede each chapter of the book. A thoughtful use of these sections (privately or in group study) will help the reader apply the findings and thoughts of the author to his or her own faith experiences and observations. Thereby a person's own journey of faith as well as the nurturing of faith in others will be illuminated.

Allan Hart Jahsmann

5

Reflecting on your faith

 The purpose of this introductory activity is to personalize the question of the first chapter. Reflecting on your own experiences of faith may help you understand the nature of faith.

So take a little time to relate the word *faith* to some key experiences in your life. The experiences need not have been "religious" in any formal sense. For example, faith may have surfaced while taking a walk through a woods. It may have been experienced at a time of great loss or suffering. An experience of faith may have occurred during a milestone event such as marriage or Confirmation. You may have been alone or with a close friend or in a group at the time.

As these past experiences of faith emerge into your consciousness, jot down three or more different occasions when you felt faith in God—faith in God's presence, power, judgment, or love. Mentally note the nature of your faith in God on each of the occasions.

Then choose one of your experiences to ponder more deeply. With your mind's eye try to reenter this experience by recalling the story that surrounds it. Who were some of the other people present? What made the occasion an important time for you? What was your impression of God in the experience? Were you afraid, sad, happy? Why? What does this memory contribute to your understanding of faith?

When the Son of Man comes, will he find faith on earth?

Luke 18:8

Chapter One
WHAT IS FAITH?

We need to understand what faith is before we can talk about how it grows and changes from one stage of life to another or from one pattern and type to another.

The Bible is our most important resource for understanding faith. So the heart of this chapter is devoted to a review of some biblical images of faith. These will serve as background for what will follow.

Psychology is another valuable source of insights into the nature of faith. Faith is a human experience, and psychology provides a variety of lenses for looking at our experiences. One such lens gives us the perspective of human development and also helps us understand stages and patterns of faith.

Chapters 2 and 3 examine two major theories of human development in terms of life and faith stages. These will be a basis for considering Christian patterns of faith from cradle to grave. But first we shall look at some of the problems in any effort to define faith.

Defining faith

Take a moment to make your own definition of faith. If you are like me, you will probably resist that suggestion. After all, you are reading this book to get answers, not to give them. But I urge you to jot down on a separate piece of paper what you think of when the word *faith* is mentioned. Keep that piece of paper handy. Later I'll ask you to refer to it. Perhaps your definition can become the beginning of a dialogue with me and with yourself as we proceed.

Every Christian knows at an intuitive level what faith is. Nevertheless, almost every Christian, including trained theologians, has a hard time defining faith. There are reasons for the difficulty. We shall explore some of the reasons by identifying problems encountered in trying to define faith.

The mystery of faith

Faith often has been called a mystery. How can we define a mystery? By mystery I do not mean that which is concealed or which cannot be known. I mean a revealed mystery: "For he has made known to us in all wisdom and insight the mystery of his will, according to his purpose which he set forth in Christ as a plan for the fulness of time" (Ephesians 1:9).

As Christians we have received by faith the revelation of God's grace in Christ, but that doesn't mean that we can define in precise terms the experience of God's grace. It remains a mystery.

If we cannot begin to describe the depths of our relationship to some human being we love deeply, is it surprising that we have trouble describing the experience of receiving the love of God and of living in communion with him?

Of course this doesn't mean we shouldn't try. It only means that we are talking about an experience for which human language seems very inadequate.

The language of faith

So how do people talk about the life of faith, the acts of believing in God? The biblical writers who described the faith of Israel or the faith of the early Christians told stories.

Those stories, in the New Testament as in the Old, depict human beings living in a faith relationship to God.

On the other hand, theologians who formulate doctrine (teachings) for the church usually offer an abstract definition in describing faith. Creeds, catechisms, and confessional statements are documents that talk about faith by means of definitions. That we confess a creed each Sunday, use a catechism as the basis for Confirmation instruction, and subscribe to a set of confessions indicates the value of those ways of talking about faith.

How do *you* usually think and talk about faith? What came to your mind when I suggested that you write down your own ideas of faith? My guess is that most of you came up with a definition rather than a story. Catechetical instruction conditioned us to do that, as well as the majority of sermons, Bible studies, and theological books we are exposed to. Many definitions; few stories.

The advantage of definitions is that they state the meaning of faith with intellectual clarity and develop an understanding of the mind. But the advantage of stories is that they invite participation in the experience of faith and offer an understanding of the heart.

Faith and experience

How important is experience for an understanding of faith? All-Important if you are telling a story. The biblical writers spoke of what they had seen and heard. When we tell our story of faith to someone else, we speak of what we have experienced. But when the pastor says, "Let us confess our faith in the words of the Nicene Creed," he or she is referring to the *content* of our faith. This "faith of the church" is independent of our experience and our confession; it has an *objective* existence or reality.

Both subjective and objective usages of the term *faith* are appropriate but quite different. The subjective meaning refers to the *experiences* of the one who believes, experiences best shared through the telling of stories. The objective meaning refers to *what* we believe, the faith content we have in common with all other Christian believers. That content can be stated in story form (as in the Gospels) or in doctrinal formulations (as in the Epistles).

Can faith be taught?

Teaching the content of faith has traditionally been a primary objective of Christian education. Christians usually have been concerned that the Word of God be taught, "the faith which was once for all delivered to the saints" (Jude 3). But there is a danger in the idea that faith can be taught. It lies in the assumption that belief and faith are the same, namely, doctrinal formulations. In this concept of faith, belief is either true or false, and one is caught in an intellectual distortion of faith. It is a distortion because belief and believing involve more than the intellect.

However, in thinking and talking about faith as experience, a very different usage of the term becomes apparent; and the question of teaching such faith changes radically. Take the story of Paul's conversion on the road to Damascus as an example. As a result of his encounter with the living Christ, Paul's life was completely changed. The purpose in sharing the story is to invite the learners to reflect on Christ's living presence and his will for themselves as well as for St. Paul.

The content of faith in this view is not a doctrine (conversion) but a person (the risen Christ) together with human responses to him. The content of faith becomes life experiences, and belief and believing become actions a person learns only by "catching" the spirit and meaning of the story.

Is faith God's doing or mine?

According to St. Paul, *Christian* faith is the work of the Holy Spirit: "No one can say 'Jesus is Lord' except by the Holy Spirit" (1 Corinthians 12:3). Luther's explanation of the Third Article of the Apostles' Creed is a commentary on this passage: "I believe that I cannot by my own understanding or effort believe in Jesus Christ, my Lord, or come to him. But the Holy Spirit has called me through the Gospel, enlightened me with his gifts, and sanctified and kept me in true faith. In the same way he calls, gathers, enlightens, and sanctifies the whole Christian church on earth, and keeps it united with Jesus Christ in the one true faith."

This emphasis on faith as God's doing fits well with what both St. Paul and Luther taught about the sinful condition of all human beings and the total inability of sinful persons to find God on their own. Only an act of God could bring human beings from death to life, from sin to grace, from being God's enemies to being restored children of God.

But though faith is not my "doing" in the sense that I can take credit for it, it is a personal experience, the experience of being in relation to him who has redeemed and transformed my life and lives in me. So it makes sense to say that faith is an act as well as a gift. It is a human act in the sense that it is I who believe even if I cannot do that "by my own understanding or effort." And the Holy Spirit has called, enlightened, and sanctified *me*. The Spirit of God is acting *in* my life, but this action is an experience and it is mine.

When does faith begin?

This is another knotty problem that has even caused divisions in the church. Luther took the position that Christian faith begins in infancy through Baptism. But "faith comes from what is heard, and what is heard comes by the preaching of Christ," said the apostle Paul (Romans 10:17). How can infants come to faith by hearing the Word of God?

There were some later dogmatists who suggested that somehow the Holy Spirit enabled the infant to hear and understand the gospel promises spoken at his or her Baptism, but that seems absurd. Luther was content to affirm that faith was necessary for any receiving of God's grace, but he attempted no rational explanation of how the infant received the necessary faith that makes Christian Baptism efficacious.

This was more than some of Luther's contemporaries could accept. They agreed that faith was necessary for Baptism to be efficacious, but they balked at the idea that infants were capable of believing. They argued that a person must not only be able to hear and understand the gospel, but must also be able to respond to that gospel. Infants are not capable of such a conscious response, so these dissenters maintained that Baptism should be postponed until a person can respond personally, not only through parents and godparents.

The psychological studies of faith stages and faith patterns considered in subsequent chapters will enable us to make some useful distinctions between the faith of infants and the faith of adults.

Traditional and revised understandings of faith

According to a traditional definition of faith, its characteristics are knowledge, assent, and trust. For many this definition implies that faith begins with knowledge, an act of the intellect. Knowledge is followed by assent, an act of the will. Assent is followed by trust, one of the more "religious" emotions. It is an emotion that is constant rather than fleeting.

Trust is the characteristic that makes Christian faith a saving faith. The traditional concept of faith has emphasized the trust element of faith. But this understanding of faith creates problems when applied to infant faith, especially if knowledge and assent are considered preconditions for trust.

Developmental classifications of faith by contemporary psychologies make it possible to reconsider the relationship of various characteristics of faith. *Instead of knowledge preceding trust, the experience of trust is seen as the beginning of faith, and knowledge becomes "faith seeking understanding."* This revised view of the characteristics of faith will be the key to our analysis of faith in the following chapters.

Bible images of faith

Having identified some of the problems we are likely to encounter as we reflect together on the meaning of faith, we turn now to resources that can help us in our study of faith. The primary resource is, or course, Scripture.[1]

Nowhere in Scripture will you find a fully developed theology of faith, but there are images of faith in Bible stories and teachings. By "images" I mean the deepest and richest expressions of human experiences.

The men who wrote the Bible were very close to events by which God revealed himself. Many were eyewitnesses. It is natural that they would rely primarily on images to communicate to others their awareness of the presence of God in their history. They expressed their faith sometimes in story form, sometimes in poetry, and sometimes in the form of declarations.

The following sections identify five key images of faith found in biblical writings.

1. In stories of Abraham

As is so often the case in the Scriptures, *stories* give us the images of faith that come from this man who is called the father of all believers (Galatians 3:7).

The story of Abraham begins in Genesis 12 after the accounts of the fall of Adam and Eve into sin, the flood, and the building of the Tower of Babel. In this time of curse and absence of faith, God called Abraham to go to a distant country, and he promised to make Abraham's descendants a nation through whom all the people of the earth would be blessed.

Abraham responded to the promise with trust and did what God told him to do. He abandoned all the ties to his people and country, a security most of us would be unwilling to give up. The only certainty Abraham had was his conviction that it was God who had spoken to him. In Abraham's obedience to that word of God we have one of the earliest biblical images of faith.

Why did Abraham believe? What gave him the faith to obey God's call? There is nothing in the story that helps us answer these questions. The narrator does not draw attention to Abraham's virtue but rather to God. Abraham was anything but a hero of faith in many of the stories that follow. It was entirely divine initiative that explains Abraham's faith.

Abraham remained childless, and that became a test of his trust in the promise that he would be the father of a great nation. Would God be faithful to his promise? Abraham was not at all certain. As he and Sarah grew old together, his great expectation slowly changed into deep resignation. He accepted the poor solution of a substitute heir. The story of Hagar and Ishmael (Genesis 16) is nothing but a human attempt to solve the problem of childlessness. So deep was Abraham's resignation that he responded to God's renewed promise of a child to him and Sarah with the outburst, "O that Ishmael might live in thy sight!" (17:18).

But for all of his doubt, Abraham remained a man of great faith. And his faith was "reckoned" by God to be righteousness (Romans 4:3, 9) because it held on to the promise of God in spite of all of the indications, like the barrenness of Sarah, that seemed to deny the fulfillment of the promise.

This faith in God's promise received its supreme test when God asked Abraham to sacrifice Isaac, his only child in whom the hope of God's promise rested. In Genesis 22 Abraham is told by God to take Isaac to a designated place in a distant region and there offer his son as a sacrifice. Unlike the earlier command which was accompanied by a promise that opened up the future, Abraham was asked to follow a command without a promise, a command which seemingly negated the promise renewed in the birth of Isaac. What was Abraham to do?

Abraham, according to the author of the Letter to the Hebrews, "considered that God was able to raise men even from the dead" (Hebrews 11:19). St. Paul speaks similarly about Abraham's faith in God "who gives life to the dead and calls into existence the things that do not exist" (Romans 4:17). Such was the radical nature of Abraham's trust in the promise of God.

The image of faith that is conveyed by these stories of Abraham is a deeply rooted trust in the promises of God, a trust that will not let go of a promise no matter how overwhelming the evidences might be against its fulfillment. I would call this the most fundamental of the biblical images of faith, the basic concept on which all other images are built.

As we shall see later, there are also developmental reasons for calling *trust* the foundational element of all faith. For now it is enough to say that in times of crisis trust will always emerge as the dominant element of a faith that is related to the promises of God.

2. In the psalms

In the psalms we find expressions of faith in the midst of suffering. The prayer life of the church, both corporate and individual, has always been rooted deeply in the language of the psalms.

What gives the expressions of faith in the psalms such power and makes them so useful in our worship to this day is their closeness to human experience. Faith as experience needs the language of experience in order to give expression to its vitality and richness. The language of the psalms is never more than a step away from human experience in its lament, its call for help in time of need, and its praise of the God who gives deliverance.

The experience of suffering is universal and can be a threat to faith. Since God is known by faith to be a loving God who wants his children to be safe and well, suffering is usually experienced as the absence of God. The Book of Job is the classic story of such an experience. But the psalms, too, are full of similar expressions of fear over a seeming remoteness of God.

"Why dost thou stand afar off, O Lord?" asks the psalmist. "Why dost thou hide thyself in times of trouble?" (10:1). "How long, O Lord? Wilt thou forget me for ever? How long wilt thou hide thy face from me?" (13:1). "My God, my God, why hast thou forsaken me? Why art thou so far from helping me?" (22:1). The temptation in such experiences is to despair, to assume that the perceived absence of God is permanent and that the faith which sustained Israel and has sustained us in the past is groundless.

But the psalmist's cry of despair is always accompanied by a search for God, a tense waiting, an expectation that God will come and save. "My soul is sorely troubled. But thou, O Lord—how long? Turn, O Lord, save my life; deliver me for the sake of thy steadfast love" (6:3–4). Here is a feeling of overwhelming trouble, but the feeling is bounded by trust in the promise and hope of deliverance.

In the psalms faith is expressed again and again in statements of trust. "Blessed is the man who makes the Lord his trust" (40:4). "For thou, O Lord, art my trust" (71:5). "O my God, in thee I trust" (25:2). "Trust in him at all times, O people" (62:8).

Psalm 23, with its shepherding metaphor, has become a favorite expression of trust in the care of God. Threat to life is depicted as a walk through the valley of the shadow of death. Imagine a shepherd and his flock walking through a ravine flanked by steep and rocky hills on either side. A late afternoon sun casts a dark shadow over the narrow path. It is the shadow of a wolf standing at the top of the ravine. But there is no fear in the sheep as they walk through this "valley of the shadow." Why? Because of the nearness of the shepherd and his protecting presence.

Trust in the Lord God, the Good Shepherd, was the bedrock of faith for the psalmist. That is particularly true also for Christians who have learned to know the love and care of God through Jesus Christ.

Praise is also an expression of faith in the psalms. It is found frequently in relation to the experience of deliverance from threat. After lamenting the absence of God in the early part of the psalm, the psalmist says: "But I have trusted in thy steadfast love; my heart shall rejoice in thy salvation. I will sing to the Lord, because he has dealt bountifully with me" (13:5–6). "How precious is thy steadfast love, O God! The children of men take refuge in the shadow of thy wings" (36:7).

The psalms are full of the praise of God: in whom our fathers trusted and were delivered (22:4), who took me from the womb and kept me safe upon my mother's breasts (22:9), who walks with me through the valley of the shadow of death (23:4). Such praise drowns the despair which threatens to cut the believer off from the source of his or her faith and life. "Why are you cast down, O my soul, and why are you disquieted within me? Hope in God; for I shall again praise him, my help and my God," the psalmist says (42:5).

The image of faith most characteristic of the psalms is the picture of a drowning person reaching for a hand that is about to deliver her or him. The threat of death is real and close, but the look of expectant hope is more prominent than the expression of fear in the face of the victim. Faith in the promise of God's love and care is experienced in the midst of suffering. It is expressed in laments colored by hope and in praise for deliverance.

3. In the prophets

The psalms are *personal* language to give expression to cries of faith in the midst of suffering. The prophets, on the other hand, speak about the faith of *Israel* in the midst of national calamity. The underlying promise of God is the same in both cases; namely, that the God of Abraham and his descendants will never forsake the people of Israel, individually or corporately. The basis of that promise in the writings of the prophets is the unconditional covenant God made with the monarchy of David and his descendants.

But the kings of Israel turned away again and again from the God Yahweh and his covenant promise. This breach of trust resulted in the fall and subsequent captivity of both the northern and the southern Hebrew kingdoms. The fundamental issue of faith for the prophets in exile was whether God can be trusted to keep his covenant even when his people have brought national disaster upon themselves by their faithlessness.

It would be hard to exaggerate the threat to their faith that the people of Israel experienced in exile. Abraham had had only the word of God on which to base his faith.

Not so his descendants. After settling in the Promised Land and establishing both a king and a Temple in Jerusalem, the people of Israel had many more signs of God's presence and promise than Abraham had.

First, there was the land of Canaan, promised to Abraham and his seed and now politically secure under the rule of a kingship. Second, there was the Temple in Jerusalem, housing the Ark of the Covenant. Above all, there was their king, through whom God had reestablished his covenant with Israel as a nation. A threat of any of these three was a threat to faith. The loss of all three was a devastating tragedy.

What was left of the faith of the Jewish people in exile? Only a hoping and waiting for the God who was now "hiding his face." It seemed to be a "strange . . . deed" and an "alien . . . work" (Isaiah 28:21) on God's part, this exile, but Israel had only one God, not two. These words in Isaiah seem very similar to the desperation voiced so frequently in the psalms. The difference is that the psalmist had high expectations of God's deliverance, while the prophet for the most part promised little more than the presence of a judging God.

Faith waits for the hidden God to show himself. Israel could no more see the future of the promise of God than could Abraham with knife poised over his son Isaac. The Babylonian Captivity was a dark night of the soul with only God's word of promise to offer a ray of light. Faith was expected to see the loving hand of God even in this catastrophe and to depend on him for salvation.

It is from this pit of Israel's history that the author of the second part of Isaiah speaks a word of comfort and hope that would not be fully realized until the coming of Christ: "Zion said, 'The Lord has forsaken me, my Lord has forgotten me.' 'Can a woman forget her sucking child, that she should have no compassion on the son of her womb?' Even these may forget, yet I will not forget you"

(49:14–15). Without any national identity remaining, Israel's hope for salvation could be grounded only in God.

But why would God save this faithless people who deserved nothing but God's judgment? "Because you are precious in my eyes, and honored, and I love you," said the prophet Isaiah (43:4). Like the love of a mother whose child could not do a wrong so great that she would turn away in hate, so God's love for Israel was as sure in the midst of its exile as it was at the height of the monarchy. Faith is clinging to God's unconditional promise of steadfast love and faithfulness.

The image of faith in the writings of the Old Testament prophets is the image of a faithless son who has squandered the family inheritance and lives in a strange land far from home. But in the background is the waiting father. The son yearns to be back home even though he can lay no claim to the love of his father.

So it is with us. The difference between us and the Old Testament people of Israel is that they had not yet experienced the full embrace of the waiting father, as did the prodigal son in the parable Jesus told. By faith in Christ Jesus we have.

4. In stories about Jesus

In the Old Testament it is through stories about Abraham that we first learn the meaning of faith. In the New Testament it is through stories about Jesus that we learn the meaning of faith. That's what the Gospels are, stories about Jesus. They are stories of faith told by a believing community in order to share the good news about Jesus Christ, crucified, dead, and risen from the dead.

The stories of Jesus invite participation in the events that unfold in the drama of his life, death, and resurrection. When he says to the paralytic, "My son, your sins are forgiven" (Mark 2:5), those words apply to us too. His dying also was for us and our sins, "and not for ours only, but also for the sins of the whole world" (1 John 2:2). In that is the promise of life.

Faith, Christian faith, is trusting in this promise of forgiveness and life. More specifically, Christian faith is trusting the person who makes the promise in the gospel story.

It is in the healing stories of Jesus' ministry that we most often find talk about faith. It is in the healing stories that Jesus most clearly reveals his identity as the Savior, as the one who makes people whole in both body and spirit. It is in the healing stories that we see the fulfillment of the promise to which Jesus referred when John the Baptizer sent two of his disciples to ask if he, Jesus, was the one who was expected to come: "Go and tell John what you have seen and heard: the blind receive their sight, the lame walk, the lepers are cleansed, and the deaf hear, the dead are raised up, the poor have the good news preached to them" (Luke 7:22).

It is in the healing stories that we see the overcoming of the powers of evil and the establishment of God's kingdom or rule. In Mark 1:15 Jesus says, "The time is fulfilled, and the kingdom of God is at hand; repent, and believe in the gospel." What follows in that first chapter of Mark are more healing accounts than are found in all of the Old Testament.

Faith gives participation in the power of God, who brings healing, forgiveness, and eternal life in the person of Jesus Christ. Healing stories are not unique to the New Testament. They are recounted in the rabbinic tradition and in the Hellenistic miracle stories. But what is unique to the Gospels is the frequently repeated statement, "Your faith has made you well" (Mark 5:34, 10:52; Luke 17:19, 18:42). In the New Testament a person turns in faith to Jesus and receives healing from him. On the other hand, when Jesus encountered lack of faith and unbelief, he performed no miraculous deeds of healing (Mark 6:6).

This does not say that faith empowers the healing. In relation to the power that effects the healing, faith is totally passive and only waits and receives. In the New Testament, faith is depicted as relational, and healing is the product of a faith relationship. Faith looks to Jesus for life and health and every good, and he grants its request.

And faith is asked to hold on to the promises of God even in the midst of a seeming negation of them. Jesus was recognized by the disciples and many others as the promised Messiah sent by God. His healings were a sign of the fulfillment of that promise. But then he was crucified. We are reminded of Isaac, son of promise, who was only a knife thrust away from what seemed to be the end of God's promise. Faith is trusting in the promise of God even when there is darkness over the face of the earth and God's Son is hanging on a cross.

Could God's promise of life survive even the horrors of this darkest moment in all of human history? The answer of faith was yes. But that was not at all obvious in the moment of its happening. The disciples needed the Resurrection and the coming of the Spirit to see the fulfillment of the promise in all that happened on Calvary.

Since then the lesson of faith is clear: no matter how enormous the sin, no matter how great the tragedy, no matter how hopeless the situation, no matter how deep the silence of God—nothing can separate us from the love of God in Christ Jesus. That was the testimony of St. Paul to the Romans (8:31–39), and it is still true for us.

Faith as trust in the promises of God reaches its highest fulfillment in the story of Jesus, dead and alive forever. We can interpret all stories of faith in the light of this supreme story.

The image of faith that emerges from this story of Jesus is the *Christus Rex* (Christ the King). It is the picture of

Jesus Christ on the cross wearing the crown of a king rather than a crown of thorns and having arms outstretched in victory rather than sagging under the agony of death. Only the eyes of faith can see through death to life, through weakness to power, through defeat to victory; but such are the eyes that trust the promises of God.

5. In the teachings of Paul

Most of us are familiar with St. Paul's use of the term *faith* because it is embedded deeply in our Christian heritage. St. Paul opposed the teaching that a person could be saved by doing works of the Law. The most prominent representatives of this false teaching in Paul's day were a group called the Judaizers. Paul's Letter to the Galatians was intended as a direct refutation of their teaching.

The Judaizers, also called the circumcision party, insisted that strict obedience to the laws of Moses was a requirement also for Christians. Paul opposed the legalists in the name of Christ and the freedom that the gospel gives to Christ's followers, Jews or Gentiles. Paul argued that "a man is not justified by works of the law but through faith in Jesus Christ" (Galatians 2:16).

Paul knew by experience what a religion of law was all about. As a Pharisee he could claim to be blameless by virtue of having achieved a kind of righteousness under law (Philippians 3:6), but he knew how easily this kind of faith led to faith in self.

Faith in self is dangerous self-deception, Paul warned, for he said the power of sin within him was greater than the power of the law with which he opposed sin. "I delight in the law of God, in my inmost self, but I see in my members another law at war with the law of my mind and making me captive to the law of sin which dwells in my members," he wrote to the Romans (7:22f).

God's answer to the problem of sin, said Paul, is the free gift of grace in Jesus the Christ (Romans 5:15–17). Jesus died for all our sins and by that act made us right with God. And there is nothing we have done, can do, or will ever be able to do that would make us worthy of this love of God: "For the wages of sin is death, but the free gift of God is eternal life in Christ Jesus our Lord" (Romans 6:23).

All of Paul's teachings revolve around this central affirmation that only God's grace frees us from the worst in ourselves and frees us for the best that God would have us be. As Christians we live from the abundance of God's gifts, at the center of which is the gift of the forgiveness of our sins.

That is the theology of Paul's writings. That is why Paul would preach nothing but Jesus Christ, dead and risen, because "he who did not spare his own Son but gave him up for us all, will he not also give us all things with him?" (Romans 8:32).

What does all this have to do with faith? For Paul, the phrase "through faith" means "by grace." Faith is the crucified and risen Jesus Christ, a faith which trusts in the assurance of God's mercy, cannot be separated from the manifestation of God's grace. And grace is entirely God's action, not ours. We can be only on the receiving end of such action.

So totally is grace God's action that Paul says, "It is no longer I who live, but Christ who lives in me; and the life I now live in the flesh I live by faith in the Son of God, who loved me and gave himself for me" (Galatians 2:20).

The image of faith most characteristic of Paul's teaching is the image of a person who has been condemned to death and is awaiting the sentence of the judge. The person is in a court of final appeal, and so there is no hope. At the last moment a person steps forward and offers to take the place of the one who has been condemned to death. The condemned person goes free, not because he or she deserves to be freed, but because of the self-sacrificing love of another.

This image of faith is to be seen in the look of surprise, of gratitude, of relief, of hope, and of new determination on the face of the person who has been freed. Such is the experience of those who by faith receive forgiveness by the grace of God in Christ and who know that there is "now no condemnation for those who are in Christ Jesus" (Romans 8:1). So profound is that experience that nothing can be imagined that "will be able to separate us from the love of God in Christ Jesus our Lord" (Romans 8.39). That's Christian faith according to St. Paul.

A working definition of faith

On the basis of our brief biblical study, we can say that *faith is trusting the promises of God.* The specific nature of the promise may vary, depending upon particular needs and historical circumstances. To Abraham the promise was descendants as numerous as the stars. To the suffering the promise is God's saving presence and help. To those in exile the promise is a new beginning in a land of promise. To the sick the promise is healing. To the sinner the promise is forgiveness. To the dying the promise is life eternal.

Despite the variety of forms, the underlying promise is always the same—that God will be present with his life-giving Spirit, his love, and his forgiveness; and will help, restore, bless, and sustain his children.

What I have described in the above paragraph and in the biblical study is what I would call the core of faith or its basic orientation. In the following pages we shall be talking about more than trust. For example, we'll talk about faith as knowing and about faith as loyalty and obedience. But at the heart of all biblical images of faith is a trusting in God's promises.

At this time compare the definition of faith as someone trusting the promises of God, with the definition you jotted down at the beginning of the chapter. What change, if any, have you made in the way you now think of faith? Try your hand at a revised definition. Write it in your book. You may want to revise it again later.

As you will see in the next two chapters, faith is an expression of the entire person. It begins early in life and continues until death. Although its foundation and continuing center is trust, faith also changes during the journey of a person's life. It will be our task to capture its nature at every stage of life. So for a further description of faith we go now to the stories of human development and their implications.

Reflecting on your development
as a person

 Whether we are twenty, forty, or eighty, a lot has happened to us since we were born, and not all of that is simply in the past. Earlier stages of our development remain a part of our total being and can surface from background to foreground with all the dominant force of the original stage.

Try to recall a tune that was popular or that you knew when you were very young. Hum that tune to yourself. If you can remember the words, sing them softly. As you do this, be aware of how you are feeling, what thoughts come to your mind, what associations you have with that song. You will very likely experience some nostalgia and a sense of reentering a time long past.

Next, close your eyes for a few minutes and recall some event or period in your life about which you have strong feelings. Instead of just thinking *about* that time, try to reenter that past experience and *be* the person you were then. If you allow yourself time for this, you will probably be able to remember what was important to you then. Picture how you looked at that time, where you lived, some of the important people in your life, what you enjoyed doing, what you wanted to do.

Now consider the following questions. Their purpose is to assist you in your reflection. Spend time with them if they are helpful. Ignore them if they're not: In what ways are you the same as you were then? How have you changed since that time in your life? Does the thought of change frighten you or excite you? What may be some of the reasons for your answer?

When I was a child, I spoke like a child, I thought like a child, I reasoned like a child; when I became a man, I gave up childish ways.

1 Corinthians 13:11

Chapter Two
FAITH TASKS AT
LIFE STAGES

The idea of *development* has come quite late in the history of ideas. Though people have always been aware of changes that take place as a person moves from childhood through adolescence, adulthood, and old age, it is only in our century that stages of the life cycle have been elaborately studied, distinguished, and defined.

We now have extensive information about biological, cognitive, and ego development. Social scientists have analyzed and charted the development of families and other social systems. There would be no graded school systems if it weren't for the profound effects that the idea of development has had in the field of education.

So it is no surprise that the church, too, has been influenced by ideas of human development and stages of growth. Church educators have applied principles of development to the preparation of graded materials for their church schools. They have emphasized that a readiness for learning unfolds in stages of increased intellectual capacities and widening social experience and that this readiness is needed also for the learning of religion.

We do not try to teach abstract doctrines to five-year-olds or expect them to understand and practice moral principles at their highest levels of justice. Most of us take these advances in educational thinking pretty much for granted and favor their application also to church education.

The Bible and psychology

So we turn now to developmental psychology for help in understanding the ways in which human beings believe, and we do so in the hope of gaining insights into the nurturing of *Christian* faith. But aren't we Christians supposed to depend on Scripture and that alone for our understanding of faith?

The Bible is certainly the primary source for understanding the nature of faith. That's why we started with a Bible study in the first chapter. And we shall continually come back to the images and definitions of faith in the Scriptures. But we can also learn about faith from sources other than the Bible.

Faith is an act of the whole person and involves psychological functions. When St. Paul said that "faith comes from what is heard" (Romans 10:17), he was talking about the psychological function of hearing and knowing.

All the language about trust, which was so dominant in our biblical study, is language about a psychological function. The trust we learn to give God is not essentially different from the trust we practice in relation to others. The way we come to know God through our hearing of the gospel is not different from the way we come to know anything else in the world.

What we learn to know and trust can, of course, be very different, and therein lies the limit to what psychology can tell us. So for a knowledge of God we look to the Scriptures as the source of the revelation of God and his will and actions. But for an understanding of *how* human beings come to know and grow in faith in that God, we can look to psychology for considerable help.

In this and the next chapter we shall examine two theories of human development that are particularly helpful in showing how faith grows throughout the life cycle. Chapter 2 is devoted to a review of the work of Erik Erikson, who traced human ego development through predictable stages of life from birth to death. Chapter 3 is devoted to the writings of James Fowler, who has distinguished and defined stages and types of knowing and valuing by which a person appropriates the content of faith.

The two theories are complementary, the first dealing with being and the second, with knowing. The first identifies the faith experiences and issues that are likely to be dominant at a particular stage of life; the second shows how such faith seeks understanding through the processes of knowing and valuing at these various ages and stages. We begin with Erikson.

Human life seasons

Erikson charts what Daniel Levinson has called the seasons of a person's life.[2] Just as there are seasons of the year, each season having its own characteristics, so there are seasons in a person's life, each with its unique life tasks. These seasons, stages, or ages, according to Erikson, are predictable in that they ordinarily come at about the same time in human growth, give or take a few years.

The seasons of a person's life are also seasons of a person's faith because faith is a component of human life. A person's faith cannot be adequately understood apart from other aspects of his or her being and life.

In addition to the idea that every person grows and matures by stages, Erikson emphasizes a proper rate and a proper sequence of growth. Each stage of human development is related to every other stage and depends on the sequential development of each previous stage. At the very beginning of human life, the Creator implanted a ground plan for the growth of the human personality.

Furthermore, though all stages exist in some form in the ground plan, a particular stage comes into focus only at its particular time of ascendancy. For example, already in the first year of life, a child will have a beginning sense of who he or she is, but it is only in late adolescence that the question of identity becomes the dominant issue.

Usually the idea of growth is that of an unfolding and a smooth transition from one stage to another, as in the growth of flowers. But according to Erikson, human development takes place only in the midst of conflict and its resolution. Erikson identified eight developmental stages, and he maintained that each stage is marked by a conflict between positive and negative forces and directions.

The conflict, according to Erikson, normally results in a crisis. Only a successful resolution of the crisis allows the personality to move into the next developmental stage with an increased sense of inner unity and an increased capacity to do well according to personal standards as well as the standards of those whose opinion the person values most.

It is almost as if a new person arises in the crisis of each stage. There is a transition period in which there is eventually a sense of both an ending and a new beginning, along with feelings of disintegration and confusion in between. What happens in the healthy personality is that a new dimension of the person, already present but not at the center of things, flowers.

Relationship of faith to life stages

Where does faith fit into this idea of human development through stages of life? As already indicated, faith is a com-

31

ponent of one's total life experience apart from which personal faith cannot be fully understood. Also in the life of a Christian, either from the time of Baptism or adult conversion, the pattern of faith will not be different from the pattern of personality development, since we are talking about one person, not two.

All this ought to be obvious, but people have a tendency to think of a person's faith as somehow separate from the rest of his or her life's experiences. Maybe that's because religion has become separated from the rest of what we are and do.

And there are some who are likely to be suspicious of faith development ideas because these ideas seem to imply that we contribute something to our salvation. Isn't this interest in religious growth, one might ask, simply an effort to determine human life with God? And doesn't any attention to the human condition deny total dependence on the workings of the Holy Spirit?

Acknowledgment of the human dimension of faith and a person's participation in such religious development need not deny the principle of justification by grace and life in Christ by the power of God's Spirit. Quite the contrary. And the ability to discern patterns of God's presence within human life can lead to a greater openness to his presence.

In his Letter to the Philippians, St. Paul spoke of his active participation in a grace that had already been given to him: "Not that I have already obtained this or am already perfect; but I press on to make it my own, because Christ Jesus has made me his own" (3:12–15). Paul worked at possessing more completely the gift he had been given; he struggled to be what he was by grace.

In what follows, the realization of the Christian life— the life of Christian faith—will be examined with the insights of developmental psychology.

32

Erikson's eight stages

We move now to a brief description of each of Erikson's eight stages in the human life cycle.[3] After the description of each stage I will comment on the part faith plays at that given stage of life in terms of human growth conditions. In later chapters we shall consider how these conditions relate to the nurturing of faith.

Stage 1. "Tell me it's O.K."

According to Erikson, the first ingredient of a healthy personality is basic trust, which is an attitude toward one's self and the world derived from the experiences of the first year of life. Basic trust is not the birthright of a child. It is a gift that is received only when the newborn infant has a parent or parent substitute who provides tender loving care and a firm sense that "all is in order."

On the security of a safe relationship between the young child and the mothering person is built all subsequent securities. Basic trust is the confidence that "somebody is there" and "that somebody loves me." This confidence is the basis for all human relationships and experience. A person needs to have those feelings of security and peace that come from those first experiences of relationship, especially when one feels tired, doubtful, alone, afraid, oppressed.

Not every experience in the first year of life evokes a feeling of trust in the child. There are times when the infant may feel abandoned, mistreated, unprotected, and totally vulnerable. From these experiences grows a sense of mistrust, a feeling that one cannot depend on others to meet the basic needs of life, especially the need for security.

Any astute observer of a child's behavior is aware of the terror that a small child can feel when separated from his or her mother or father. When the fund of basic mistrust is greater than the supply of basic trust, a feeling of estrangement can result in later years. The most extreme form of such a state is displayed by individuals who regress into psychotic behavior rather than run the risk of trusting anyone. The crisis of trust and mistrust, though of major importance during the first year of life, persists throughout life.

Erikson saw the need for religion to undergird a person's sense of trust. Awareness of the presence of God fosters a sense of trust. On the other hand, awareness of the power of evil fosters a sense of mistrust. This indicates how important faith in a powerful, loving God is for overcoming the life experiences of evil.

Our study of biblical images of faith in the first chapter supports Erikson's basic psychological observation that trust is at the very center of the experience of faith. We shall devote Chapter 4 to a further analysis of trust as the fundamental element of faith.

Stage 2. "Let me do it!"

The achieving of autonomy is the second major task in human development. This occurs when the helpless infant of the first stage becomes an active youngster who can crawl or toddle around the room and feels secure enough to do so. Ready to explore and learn, the child of two years tries to handle everything. This is the beginning of what will become its adult will.

At the second stage there are no inner controls for this burgeoning assertiveness. The child's insistence on doing things his or her own way can be very annoying to those who feel responsible for the child. Ask any parent about the "terrible twos" and you will be flooded with stories about the two-year-old's demanding drive for independence.

Even parents who are dedicated to allowing their children freedom to discover their abilities and their world must set some limits. In a battle of wills which often ensues, *no* becomes the most frequently used word by both the parent and the child. But when parents are too quick to set limits and too stern with their no, their child develops feelings of doubt and shame.

The demand of a parent or teacher for total obedience and perfect control crushes the growing "plant" before it has an opportunity to take root. A firmly developed and continued stage of early trust is particularly important for the nourishment of the fragile human will. The infant's basic security and trust, which is the lasting treasure gained in the first stage of life, must not be jeopardized by the developing wish to make choices. A child who insists on "doing it *my* way" needs to be undergirded by a rich measure of trust in both the self and its surrounding world.

The emergence of the human will has implications for religious development, particularly in relation to the role of obedience in faith. The counterpart to the rules of parents is the law of God. Our experience with the law of God is often as negative as the child's experiences with the rules of parents.

It is a maxim among Lutherans that "the law always accuses." The law is like a mirror that reveals our sins. It creates a sense of shame and doubt not unlike what a two-year-old feels under a constant barrage of an accusing no, no, no from a parent. This is the experience of a person who is estranged from God and in need of forgiveness. To use traditional Lutheran language, the law precedes the gospel and ought be used only in conjunction with the gospel.

On the other hand, the forgiven sinner can be an obedient child of God. The obedience of faith is an obedience rooted in trust and expressed in love. When a child confronts his or her parent's will outside of a positive relationship, the parent's will becomes a condition of the child's worth and so a threat. But when the will of the parent (or substitute parent) is seen within a positive relationship, the child is able to obey willingly.

So it is in a person's relation to God. The will of God is a threat only when we are estranged from God. Within a positive relationship of love and trust—of faith—the will that we are called upon to obey is indeed another will than ours. But we find our selfhood by being willing to obey God's will.

Stage 3. "I am what I can imagine I will be."

Having gained a sense of being on their own, children must find out what kind of persons they can become. Beyond the increased capacity for freedom of movement and use of language, the most striking development in the child of ages four to six is an expanded imagination that permits the child to do things in fantasy that are quite impossible in reality.

Not only is the imagination of most young children richer than that of the adults they encounter, but they also do not make the clear distinctions between fantasy and reality that adults automatically make all the time. Thus, when children imagine what they will be, they have in some sense already become what they imagine.

A child who has not been crushed by the no, no, no of the previous period becomes more loving, more relaxed, and more eager to please the adults in his or her life. Most of all, such a child is prepared to take initiative, striving for accomplishment and responsibility. It is this feeling of initiative which becomes the basis for a realistic sense of ambition and purpose. As children succeed at tasks, they get a good feeling about themselves and feel that the world is basically a good place.

The belief that there is meaning and purpose and value in life, all of which have their roots in this stage, needs to be grounded in a theology of the created goodness of the universe. It is easy to get so preoccupied with the fall of humankind into sin and the evil which has spread into every nook and cranny of the world that we fail to see the beauty of the world in which a third-stage child can take such delight. A child needs to feel that "I am what I can imagine God wants me to be."

A Stage 2 sense of initiative needs to be developed by the feeling that there is purpose and goodness in the larger order of things and that we ought to strive to become the kind of people God wants us to be. The sense of initiative begins very early, as Erikson reminds us, and its healthy growth depends largely on the beliefs and attitudes of parents. If they believe in an ordered universe that is grounded in a good and gracious God, their children will feel freer to take the initiative to be what they imagine God wants them to be, even at the risk of failure.

The danger of this third stage is that the sense of initiative a child feels may lead to acts for which the child is not ready and which may be perceived by both the child and others as evil or bad. Since the child of this age does not make clear distinctions between fantasy and reality, he or she, through initiative plus imagination, can use considerable power to do the very worst.

Add to that the innumerable times when the child's initiative is thwarted or his or her accomplishments are ignored and berated, and you have fertile ground for feelings of guilt and failure to grow, sometimes to the point where there is room for nothing else. Fortunately most children in this stage are so busy initiating new areas of interest and activity that they have little energy left for guilt caused by mistakes or incompleted tasks.

But Erikson tells us that the roots of the conflict between a sense of initiative and a sense of guilt can be traced back to this developmental stage. When surrounded by a community of people who mediate the unconditional love of God, children are usually able to resolve the crisis of this period with a favorable balance of initiative over guilt.

Stage 4. "I really can do it!"

At no time is the child more ready to learn quickly and avidly than at the end of the period of expanding imagination. In this fourth stage (roughly age 6 to 12) children are ready to attach themselves to teachers. They will watch and imitate people in occupations they know—firefighters, doctors, police, and sports heroes.

In short, they are ready to learn things and make things, to think and to do. Erikson calls this a sense of industry. Without it even the best-entertained child feels unfulfilled. The roots of a productive personality are found in this fourth stage.

The danger or crisis at this stage of development is a sense of inferiority, the feeling that "I can't do anything well." This may be caused by an inadequate solution to the preceding conflict. A child who cannot take the initiative to complete tasks is not likely to develop a feeling of competence. This stage is particularly important in a society which places a heavy emphasis on proper schooling for children and on productivity for adults.

An overemphasis on productivity as a criterion for worth in our society has produced in most of us a feeling that our value is dependent on the quality and quantity of our work. This can and does contribute to a deeply imbedded tendency to believe that we are saved by our works. While we need to foster a sense of industry in our children, we must be careful not to suggest that their worth as our children and as children of God is linked to their successes or failures.

Stage 5. "Who am I?"

Erikson has popularized the term *identity*, which is the central developmental issue for adolescents. The quest for identity often extends into young adulthood. It is a quest for a sense of inner consistency and continuity matched by a consistency and continuity in what one means to others. The formation of identity reaches a crisis point during adolescence, when a person either "grows together" into a self or fails to "get it all together" in an integrated and consistent whole.

The roots of identity go all the way back to the time when the infant gets a dim awareness of who he or she is in the mirror of a parent's face. Already in this early stage of development a child is told who he or she is. "You are a person who eats with a spoon, wears clothes, goes to church," and so on. At the time of adolescence the individual is forced into choices which either confirm or negate the identity that has been given, thus leading to a more stable self-identification, to irreversible role patterns, and to basic commitments for life.

Erikson uses the word *confirmation* to describe the way in which the wider community recognizes and solidifies the identity of youth. This can be either positive or negative. The adult world confirms the delinquent as well as the individual who assumes an acceptable role. The confirming process, however, is a mutual one. Youth has the power to confirm those who confirm them. They do this by their responses and actions, telling their elders whether the life models represented by the older generation have meaning for them.

As identity formation takes place, young people develop a growing self-assurance. Out of this personal confidence they are able to make decisions which are uniquely their own. This growing self-identity along with a capacity for fidelity makes commitment possible. Fidelity is the ability to stick with one's commitment in spite of competing loyalties.

The meaning of faith in terms of identity can be defined as the sense of consistency and continuity that one has as a loved child of God. Our identity as children of God is rooted in our Baptism, but there are many occasions throughout childhood when parents and others confirm that identity.

That confirming process for Christian identity reaches a culmination in the liturgical rite of Confirmation. Ideally at that time a young person should be able to make a personal commitment and pledge of fidelity. This has always been thought of as one meaning of faith. Whether most early adolescents are ready to make this commitment is still a question.

But for the process of confirmation to be complete, a commitment of faith is necessary. If the Christian faith is to be one's own, a personal decision for it must be made, even though the commitment may be lacking a dramatic moment and self-consciousness. In a sense confirmation of faith is going on all of the time, one's personal identity being both a gift and a personal commitment. But the commitment, either for or against, is crucial in the identity crisis.

Stage 6. "With this ring I thee wed."

The conflict that faces young adults is intimacy versus isolation. By the word *intimacy* Erikson wants to suggest the deepest kind of bond that can exist between a person and another person, or between a self and an idea or cause.

Erikson insists that true intimacy, sexual or otherwise, is impossible until one is sure of his or her own identity. Before the "two shall become one" each must be a fully centered self.

Love is the virtue, or human strength, which emerges out of this stage when the developmental issue is resolved positively. Erikson contends that genuine love, in the sense that one can give of him- or herself without fear of loss of self, is literally impossible until this stage of life.

The counterpart of intimacy is isolation—the readiness to repudiate and, if necessary, destroy those people and ideas that appear to be dangerous. Thus the failure to achieve intimacy has as a lasting consequence the readiness to use any weapon, including religion, to destroy that which threatens me. The problem is how to love another person while still loving one's self, how to be interdependent without losing one's independence, how to give and still receive.

The implications of this stage for faith are related to the practice of Christian fellowship. We regularly speak of the church as the communion of saints and the family of God. Fellowship, and the intimacy which that implies, is at the core of our understanding of the church. We become family members in the church from the time of our Baptism, but we grow only gradually into an awareness of what that means. It is at this stage of life that there is readiness for the intimacy that full participation in the church implies.

What is true for the church is eqully true for Christian marriage and family life. People need help in dealing with issues of intimacy throughout life. But it is especially important that young adults secure the foundations of their personal and family life in the warmth of Christ's presence and love; for only through a loving spirit can intimacy grow and feelings of isolation be avoided.

Stage 7. "Beloved, let us love one another."

Among the life-cycle stages that Erikson differentiates, the one covering the longest time span is middle adulthood, roughly from the early thirties to the middle sixties. Generativity versus stagnation is the crisis that Erikson identifies for this period. The word *generativity* refers to the desire to produce and nurture children. But it also refers to all that a person might produce and leave behind.

Care is the human virtue that emerges in this stage of development. Parents must be able to nurture their children's capacity to trust as well as their sense of autonomy, competence, and identity, for all these equip their children to become grown-ups and parents.

But the term *care* applies to all that adults produce for this and future generations. Human beings who have few opportunities or challenges to care for others through what they create or do are likely to experience a sense of stagnation. This feeling is the greatest threat of this period in a person's life.

The tension between generativity and stagnation, which can be expected to precipitate a developmental crisis in the healthiest of environments, has become great in our age of high technology and rising divorce rates. Parents who are separated from their children and workers who are separated from the products lose much of their capacity to care and often become psychologically impoverished and bored.

The faith implications of crisis in this stage are obvious. Genuine Christian faith, when it matures, becomes active in love, as St. John reminds us throughout his Gospel and epistles. A Christian's caring for others is an extension of Christ's caring. Jesus' spirit of caring was vividly expressed in his concern for the future of Jerusalem when he said tearfully, "How often would I have gathered your children together as a hen gathers her brood under her wings, and you would not!" (Matthew 23:37).

Diakonia is the Greek term in the New Testament that comes closest to the idea of religious generativity. Meaning service or ministry, *diakonia* is caring for others in the countless ways in which the needs of others are met.

The Christian who does not grow in caring concern and actions has a faith that is stagnating or dead. As James put it, "Faith by itself, if it has no works, is dead" (James 2:17).

Caring concern is also at the heart of the church's mission as it reaches out to the lost, the needy, and the oppressed people of the world. Christ's proclamation of the coming kingdom of God is the Christian dream of a just and caring society and a world at peace.

Stage 8. "If I should die before I wake . . ."

There comes a time in life when that popular evening prayer of childhood becomes an honest expression of faith rather than a cause for anxiety. Erikson suggests that it is possible to face death without anxiety if one can look back on life with a sense of integrity rather than despair.

Has my life had value for me and others? Were the benefits to me and others worth the struggle? Such questions a person must be able to answer in the affirmative in order to complete the life cycle with a sense of satisfaction and completeness, says Erikson.

But integrity so defined does not locate the chief task of faith at this stage of life. Christians find peace and hope at the end of life in a faith that promises forgiveness and eternal life as a gift of God's grace.

It is significant that, in explaining the last stage of the life cycle, Erikson does not speak about trust. For him there is nothing left to trust other than the good one leaves behind. That offers little comfort when death means loss of everything.

Trust, and the hope which flows from it, is the dominant element of Chistian faith at the end of human life, even as it was in the beginning, and helplessness is a condition that calls for trust.

As death approaches, Christians trust in Christ. They say with Paul, "Whether we live or whether we die, we are the Lord's" (Romans 14:8b). To the person for whom Jesus Christ has been the eternal presence of God throughout life, Jesus promises a continuation of that presence also in death.

Reflecting on changes in your faith

 How did you come to know what you now believe? Obviously your faith has not always been entirely the same as it is now. In what respect has it changed? What contributed to the changes? The following activity will help you reflect on how your thinking has changed in what you believe and what may have caused the changes.

Our basic beliefs change over a period of time because our capacity to understand changes as we grow. Consider the doctrine of the creation of the world. Try to recall the earliest picture you had of God creating the world. Then trace the development of your thinking about the creation of the universe since that time. When did some shifts take place? Have the changes been a strengthening or a weakening of your faith—or perhaps both? Do you anticipate further changes in your faith in the future? Why or why not?

Lutherans frequently are encouraged to remember their Baptism because their Christian faith is strengthened through such remembering. What do you think of when you "remember" your Baptism? An explanation? An image? A story? An experience? A promise? How is that remembrance similar to and different from what you probably thought when you were confirmed?

If you have time, do the same kind of reflecting on your Confirmation, the Lord's Supper, your purpose in life, and particularly on what you think God has in mind for you. What did you believe in the past? What do you presently think? What caused any changes in your thinking?

The apostles said to the Lord, "Make our faith greater."

Luke 17:5, TEV

Chapter Three
FAITH SEEKING UNDERSTANDING

In the previous chapter we examined characteristics of faith related to sequential stages of the human life cycle. In this chapter we shall consider patterns or characteristics of faith at stages of thinking and knowing.

James Fowler, following a school of thought developed by Jean Piaget and Lawrence Kohlberg, is the leader in a growing field of research on faith patterns of thinking and knowing. We will rely on his theory, the product of empirical studies, for our study of faith seeking understanding.

Types of knowing

Piaget demonstrated that the mental activity of human beings develops in a sequence of discernible, distinguishable stages, each stage being a set of mental operations used by a person in thinking about a particular subject matter. According to Piaget, the mind operates in an orderly fashion regulated by given ways of organizing information and knowledge at any particular point in the person's life.

At whatever stage of mental development, human beings sort through the information that comes to them from both inside and outside the body. Processing that information means determining what can be incorporated into the self, what must be ignored, and how the information that is accepted can be interpreted and organized so as to make sense.

A number of years ago I was watching a football game on television. My daughter, who was then three years old, commented, "Boomps go the boys!" That expression was her interpretation of the event, given the mental structure with which she processed what she had observed. Piaget traces the growth of mental capacities and ways of thinking to four distinct stages.

Kohlberg applies Piaget's principles to the making of moral judgments. He assumes that moral judgments have a rational basis similar to intellectual judgments, and he has devised a theory of moral development that presents a sequence of stages like those of Piaget. Each of these stages is characterized by a distinguishable pattern of thought or reasoning used by a person in making a moral judgment.

For example, a young child will think that breaking four glasses accidentally is much worse than breaking one on purpose. The criterion the young child uses for judgment is the amount of damage done, not the intent of the person.

Fowler has searched for a similar set of stages in the thinking and knowing that is related to faith. However, his research differs from both Piaget and Kohlberg in that he is probing for a deeper and broader kind of knowing than Piaget and Kohlberg have analyzed.

Knowing in faith

Before we look more closely at Fowler's research, we need to define what we mean by the knowing part of faith. At its deepest level faith is a relationship of trust and loyalty to the God who promises love and life. That relationship can and does exist apart from conscious awareness or intellectual comprehension. An infant, for example, receives the blessings of Baptism through a faith which has no intellectual dimension to it, and faith obviously does not stop when we go to sleep. We do not have to think about faith in order to have it.

However, we do think about our faith. We form images, concepts, and doctrines to express the faith we have, to share it with one another in worship and other communal activities, and to pass it on to others in teaching and witnessing. As one of the ancient maxims of the church puts it, "Faith seeks understanding." Faith, our experience of trust and loyalty in relation to God, seeks images and concepts that will express, within the limits of human reason, an understanding of this relationship.

Faith-knowing is faith seeking understanding. The way we know God in faith is not different from the way we know other persons and objects in our environment. Knowing is a product of interacting with our environment. God discloses himself as loving and merciful through the Bible, the sacraments, the liturgy, and through other Christians. Knowing takes place when we use our reason to understand and express the significance of God's love and actions in our lives.

At its deepest levels, faith forms powerful images of God's gracious activity. We might call them images of grace and promise. There will likely be much feeling and emotion attached to such images.

The adequacy of the images can be judged by comparing them with the master images we find in Scripture and tradition, images like the heavenly Father, the kingdom of God, the good shepherd, the great physician. Beyond images, faith forms stories, concepts, and doctrines, the truth of which can be tested by the norm of the Scriptures.

The main point of the above discussion is that the knowledge of faith, *what* we believe, is not just something given in the form of doctrines, ecclesiastical and parental pronouncements, or tradition to be received passively by the knower. Our minds do not receive the contents of our faith as a clean sheet of paper receives the printing of a typewriter.

That is one concept of indoctrination, literally the pouring in of doctrine. But in "faith as knowing"—the "I *know* whom [and what] I have believed" of St. Paul (2 Timothy 1:12)—the mind is actively engaged in forming the contents by means of thinking. This thinking is done in patterns. (Fowler calls them mental structures.) These patterns can and do change in predictable, developmental stages.

We all know that children will think about God in different ways at different ages, even though what we tell them about God is essentially the same. That's because their patterns of seeing and knowing the world (including God) change. At every age there may be a firm grasp of the promises of God and responses of trust and loyalty, but how God is conceived will change as a person matures and the mind develops.

Charting the changes

Is there a way of charting those changes in ways of thinking and knowing? That's the question Fowler brought to interviews with persons of faith. He was able to distinguish consistent patterns in their characteristic ways of believing, patterns that follow a developmental sequence.

Six different faith patterns, called stages of faith by Fowler, parallel rules or laws that the mind follows in reasoning. Each of these stages has its place within a sequential order. The sequential order is invariant, meaning that, as in the growth of a flower, the sequence of stages never varies. No stage can ever be skipped.

Furthermore, each new stage builds on and incorporates into its more elaborate pattern the operations of the previous stage. This means that development from one stage to the next is always in the direction of greater complexity and flexibility.

It is for this reason that the more developed stages can be considered more adequate and in some sense "more true" than the less developed stages. They can be said to be more adequate, even though the most highly developed forms of knowing fall far short of complete or perfect comprehension of God's power, justice, and love.

Growth from one stage to the next is not automatic and not as directly related to age as are the stages in the life-cycle theory. Biological maturation, chronological age, psychological development, and mental age are all factors that affect the readiness to make a stage transition. Transitions occur when the stability of a given stage is weakened by crises, new disclosures, and challenges that stretch the person's present pattern of faith.

The transitions between stages are critical junctures (crises) at which a person's life of faith can be severely threatened. A stage transition means a painful ending as well as a new beginning. It means giving up a total way of making sense of things. It frequently entails confusion, doubt, uncertainty, and what may appear as a loss of faith.

Thus it is not surprising that we cling to one way of thinking in our faith-life, even when this proves to be constricting and distorted. Fowler's research indicates that resistance to growth in faith happens often with many people remaining at Stages 2 or 3 during their entire lifetime.

Stages not good or bad

Before taking a closer look at each of the stages, it is important to remember that a particular *pattern* of thinking determines the stage of knowing (also in matters of faith) and not the *content* of the person's faith. People with widely different theological positions may share a common stage of knowing. At the same time two people who make the same biblical or doctrinal affirmation may employ two different ways of thinking about it. For this and other reasons to be given later, it would be a serious mistake to use these stages as a basis for giving people good or bad "grades" in faith.

On the other hand, parents and teachers will find it helpful to understand *how* people think as well as *what* they think, especially in matters of faith. Such understanding will make it easier to help others think more appropriately about God, themselves, and life with God, and "to grow up in every way . . . into Christ" (Ephesians 4:15).

Stages of faith

Stage 1. "God's just like my mommy and daddy."

Children at this stage (age range from two to six) may never make that statement, but the way they think about God will be greatly affected by their relationship to their parents—the biggest, most powerful people in the world. It is the parents who promise protection and nurture, not so much by what they say but by acting as persons in control. Thereby they provide a young child's first idea of what God may be like.

A young child cannot but be impressed at seeing his or her mother and father addressing God with respectful devotion. "You mean there's someone even bigger and more powerful and better able to take care of me than Dad or Mom? Wow!" It's not easy for a young child to differentiate between parents and God, to say where a parent stops and God begins. That's why a child's mental pictures of God are so strikingly similar to the persons with authority in his or her life.

The imagination of preschool children is rich and fanciful. Unrestrained by logical thought, the child's imagination runs freely and is easily engaged by fairy tales, biblical narratives, cartoons—any and all stories that begin to give shape to its experiences of the world. And the experiences also include all kinds of terrors—lions, monsters, ghosts, and "things that go bump in the night."

The knowing adult may reassuringly say, "Now, now, don't be afraid; there really are no such things around." But there really are such things around in the imagination of the child, a powerful imagination that is quite unimpressed by the adult's rational explanations.

Preschool children simply do not have the capacity to make the distinctions between what is real and what is fantasy. Furthermore, they take for granted that what they see and imagine is the only way it could be. To ask them to see things from a rational perspective is to ask them to do what they are not capable of doing.

The images of God that a child begins to form at this stage do not fit together in a coherent pattern. That's not surprising when you stop to think that he or she cannot even follow the story line in a movie. Brief episodes can create powerful impressions, but in the young child's mind there is no larger framework within which to fit the concrete images coming into the mind.

To put this in another way, a preschooler's thinking is magical and fluid. Each child puts together fragments of stories and images that fit his or her needs.

The responsiveness of children to images and stories that evoke both fear and trust suggests that their teachers ought to be seriously concerned about the kind of stories and images they provide as food for their children's fertile imaginations.

This doesn't mean that all the stories have to be light and cheerful. The scary stories in fairy tales and some biblical narratives can provide media that help the young child externalize inner anxieties. For example, young children identify with dragon and Goliath slayers who are able to do what they feel powerless to do.

But adults need to remember what is at stake for the child whose smallness and powerlessness make him or her very vulnerable to the worst things that big people might do and often do to them. For such children the issue is survival.

Above all, the child needs to be sure of the parents' promise to provide care, protection, and nurture, no matter what—no matter how big the enemies are "out there" or how bad and undeserving the child might be. This first stage is fertile ground indeed for the beginning of long-lasting images of both God and Satan.

All of us, no matter how mature and rational we have become, still have within us images that were born in this period of our lives. Those images, which have very likely been reshaped over time, still exert a powerful influence in our lives, especially in periods of crisis. We all have times of powerlessness when only the images of God's protective power and caring presence enable us to live and grow.

At such times what we need is a God who is *Abba*, meaning father, a God who is able to be and do what only *Abba* can do. To such a God we can respond not only with trust but also with love and obedience, willing to follow wherever he may lead, no matter how filled with shadows and terrors that way may be.

Stage 2. "What's fair is fair!"

One of the characteristics that distinguishes school-age children (ages seven to twelve) from preschoolers is the emergence of the idea of fairness. The preschool child has no basis for distinguishing right from wrong other than the authority of parents. What is wrong is what displeases the parent, like spilling milk, hitting your sister, and breaking things. The more damage you do, the greater the wrong, whether you did it on purpose or not.

In Stage 2 a sense of fairness comes into play: "You get what you deserve (or you ought to) from parents, from others, and from God." But that's not an abstract principle for a child; it's a concrete way to bring order into the world, to know what to expect, and to insure fair treatment. If there's a piece of cake to be divided between two children at this stage, you'd better have a plan for making the action a fair one, like saying, "Mary, you divide the cake and Joe will get first choice."

Another characteristic of the school-age child is the telling of stories about school, playmates, and current adventures. These stories, which can tax the patience of the most attentive of parents, are the way Stage 2 children make sense out of their world. Stories for the Stage 1 child provide avenues for the expression of feelings and the formation of images, but the preschool child does not yet generate stories. The stories of Stage 2 children, who separate the real from the unreal, give meaning and value to their experiences.

Generally these stories will be quite "flat" and are meant to be taken literally. The actors in the religious stories of this stage are anthropomorphic, including God, who may be described as an old man with a flowing white beard.

Indeed, children of this age are much more likely to think of God in anthropomorphic ways than children in Stage 1. The reason for this is the new-found ability of children at Stage 2 to accept the perspective of others. In other words, they can think of what God might be like as distinct from themselves and others they know.

The stories Stage 2 children tell are not yet abstract reflections about themselves, God, or the world. If the flow of life is compared to a stream, we might say that a child at Stage 2 describes the flow from the middle of the stream. But he or she is not yet capable of stepping out of the stream and reflecting on the stories about the "flow of life" and the meaning of it. Interpretation requires the capacity to make abstractions, and this ability awaits the coming of the next stage.

The characteristics of Stage 2 help to explain why simple stories about good and evil are so popular at this age and often throughout life. I used to look forward all week to the Saturday matinee and the Westerns I saw there week after week. The good guys always won out in the end, and evil received its due. This was as close to absolute truth as I came at that time. Soap operas and standard television fare capture the attention of so many Americans because much of Stage 2 remains in all of them.

Law and *gospel* are two of the most useful terms we have for describing how God acts toward us. At Stage 2 law stories will have the greater appeal. In such stories God is likely to appear as our judge and we as the condemned. Such imagery of God appears throughout Scripture and in the church's tradition.

The Book of Job is a classic story of a man who struggled against a view of the world and God that said the righteous prosper and the evil suffer—that we all get what we deserve. Luther lived in an age when the fear of judgment and the promise of reward were strong. The limitations of this stage are those of a theology of law. It can result in a pervasive sense of badness and in efforts at self-righteousness.

To present the gospel as trustable promise is the challenge for teachers and parents of children at this stage. Some stories in the gospel are likely to be difficult to present as gospel because they seem so patently unfair; for example, the Parable of the Workers in the Vineyard who all received the same pay even though some worked much longer than others. Stories like the Parable of the Prodigal Son, who got what he deserved for squandering his inheritance but was welcomed back by a loving father, have a better chance of being heard by persons in Stage 2 thinking.

Stage 3. "I believe what the church believes."

The transition from Stage 2 to Stage 3 normally begins by about age 12. Some persons may begin to develop out of Stage 3 by age 18. For many it comes later, and a significant number of adults remain at Stage 3 throughout their lives.

Remaining there is not necessarily bad. Stage 3 provides a protentially stable and well-organized pattern of thinking by means of which adults can maintain a meaningful faith and life. There are also many institutions in our society, including the church, that reinforce Stage 3 thinking in their members.

Stage 3 is a conformist stage in that what Stage 3 people believe is deeply influenced by the expectations and judgments of others. Such persons have difficulty in saying why they believe what they believe.

A good example of how such faith is formed is the traditional process of Confirmation instruction. The Catechism contains both questions and answers. Ordinarily the confirmand is not expected to generate independent questions and certainly not independent answers.

At Stage 3 there will be little or no resistance to this process of indoctrination as long as the authority of the church is supported by a consensus of "significant others" in the confirmand's life—parents, the pastor, friends. In ethnic communities of earlier days, there were rarely any problems with this process of confirming the adolescent in the faith of the family and the church. The person's faith had its beginning in the confirmand before he or she was aware of what it might mean to be a Christian.

In a cohesive society where significant roles (place in the family, membership in church, social class, occupation) were clearly defined and taken for granted, one could grow through Stage 3 faith formation without a hitch. It is not that simple for most adolescents in our increasingly pluralistic society. They are likely to be surrounded by people whose expectations and judgments differ.

Both adolescents and adults at Stage 3 are likely to choose one of two strategies to resolve the dilemma of conflicting authorities. One strategy is to act one way with peers and another way with parents, which works well unless both peers and parents happen to be together. Another strategy is to elevate one authority over the rest, for example, making peers and their values most important and subordinating all other authorities to them.

Why is it important to conform to the expectations of others at Stage 3? Because at Stage 3, persons develop the capacity for seeing themselves as others see them. This is a revolutionary event in interpersonal relations, made possible by a new level of thinking.

You will remember that at Stage 2 persons tell stories that express the meaning of their lives from within the flow of the stream of their lives. At Stage 3 these same persons can step outside the flow of that stream and reflect on the patterns and meanings which they see in the stream.

What's more, they can compose images of themselves as they might be or as others see them. Fowler stated a couplet that aptly expresses this new development in thinking: I see you seeing me; I see the me I think you see. Suddenly the adolescent believes everyone is looking at him or her and becomes terribly concerned that the me they see is OK.

At this stage there is a deep hunger for acceptance by those whom the adolescent values. There is a deep religious hunger for a God who knows, accepts, and confirms people in spite of all their inadequacies, faults, limitations, and failures.

The development of the capacity to see yourself as others see you also makes it possible to see yourself mirrored in the response of others to you. The intense personal relationship between "best friends" and "first loves" is not yet the intimacy of mutual interrelatedness, but rather the discovery of one's identity in the mirror of another person's response. The religious dimension of such mirroring is the discovery of who you are as God sees you. At its best, this is what identity formation in Confirmation instruction is all about.

A person at Stage 3 will be attracted to an image of a God who is deeply personal and affirming. In this image God is perceived as being a friend, a companion, a counselor, or a guide. Qualities of love, caring, and support are central in such an understanding of God. At a stage when significant others are terribly important for the formation of a person's sense of identity, God is potentially the most significant other in the forming of that identity.

At Stage 3 faith remains unexamined. A person can be very articulate about the images and values he or she holds and can feel strongly about them but still be unable to think critically about them. Reliance on external authority is needed for the forming and sustaining of a basic faith. Such reliance is encouraged by a confession of faith to which members of a Christian community are expected to confirm.

For many Christians there is no growth in faith beyond this point. But for some who are exposed to a critical examination of their faith in the light of alternative points of view either inside or outside the community, there may be readiness for a transition to Stage 4.

Stage 4. "As I see it, God is . . ."

I teach in the theology department of a Lutheran university. For the most part students come to the university from fairly conventional and parochial communities. These are ideal settings for Stage 3 formations of faith. Though the university community provides an environment that has many points of continuity with their parochial backgrounds, incoming students are challenged by new ways of thinking about the world and God, both in the classroom and through interaction with students from differing backgrounds.

For most of the students (though certainly not for all) this shift in location from home to university is matched by a readiness on their part for a shift from a Stage 3 to a Stage 4 way of thinking. This shift is precipitated by the realization that other authorities argue for their values and beliefs as convincingly as the earlier authorities argued for theirs.

At first this discovery may result in a shift of allegiance to new authorities who supposedly know the truth. The shift does not work well for very long, though, because the student soon discovers that the new authorities often clash with each other in what they value and believe to be true. A period of confusion and distrust of all authorities often follows.

But over a period of years mature students are able to assume the responsibility for making their own judgments. There is a movement from conformity to individuality, from strongly felt but unexamined trust and loyalty to objective reflection on different points of view, from being what others want them to be to being the person they are and can become. This is the shift from Stage 3 to Stage 4. Admittedly people oscillate between the stages while maturing from one stage to the next.

I have used the example of a student going to college because that is where I observe the shift from Stage 3 to 4 most often and because it is a particularly good environment for facilitating the shift. This facility in growth is one of the best reasons I can give for sending children to college, particularly a church-related college.

There are other ways to leave home, of course, even when one stays in the same house. Associations with fellow workers, social relationships, and community organizations are some of the ways in which contact can take place with people whose values and points of view may differ widely from one's own.

The best time for faith to mature is during young adulthood. Such development is a natural accompaniment to leaving home and making a beginning at finding a place in the world. Stage 4 is a much more difficult transition for someone in his or her late thirties or early forties, because by that time the expectations of both the self and others have become set.

The perceptive reader will probably have noted a close relationship between Stages 3 and 4 on the one hand and the life-cycle task of identity formation on the other. It might be well to reread the section on identity formation at this point.

Both Stages 3 and 4 are closely related to the formation of an identity. In Stage 3 the identity is given; and in Stage 4 it is made one's own. Ideally the transition from Stage 3 to Stage 4 of faith would take place within that stage of the life cycle called identity formation.

Throughout most of childhood a person's identity is necessarily a gift from others. Children are dependent on parents for almost everything during the early formative years, including all their basic values and beliefs. Parents do not ask their children if they want to eat with a knife and fork, wear clothes, go to school, or attend church. It is only in late adolescence or early adulthood that a person is ready to make a given identity his or her own or begins the task of fashioning a new identity for which he or she can assume full responsibility. A transition from Stage 3 to 4 is necessary before either kind of identity can develop.

The content of faith may not shift at all in a person's faith-growth from Stage 3 to Stage 4. Keep in mind the distinction between structure and content. *How* one thinks about what one believes can change even though the *contents* of the faith remain the same. An entire congregation can confess together the same creed, even though there is a wide variety of life-cycle and thought stages represented by the individual believers.

At Stage 4 there will be a preference for propositions over poetry, for explicit meanings over rich symbols, for abstract knowledge over a sense of mystery. This is as much loss as gain, even for those who are committed to the quest for clear and explicit meanings. Many who have had rich religious experiences that cannot be contained within the neat but sterile categories of a Stage 4 faith grow restless with the flatness of Stage 4 thinking and knowing. It is in the restlessness that we see the readiness for a transition to Stage 5.

Stage 5. "Don't confuse the map with the territory."

One of the purposes of our thinking is to provide us with a map—call it an image or a picture—of what we experience. So it is also in our faith-thinking. Scripture, theological doctrines, and hymns are all maps charting and presenting the experiences of people who have received the revelation of God, the Word of the Lord.

Stage 4 believers want the map to be as true and clear as it can be, with boundaries carefully drawn and everything neatly in place. In Stage 5 it is as if the believer leaves the map and returns to the territory that the map has charted, the territory being the experiences that are the very "stuff" of faith.

Stage 5 persons discover that their maps are not only incomplete and limited in capturing the depth and beauty of the landscape, but they also sense that something in addition to maps is needed to put one in touch with the fullness of what has been revealed. With that discovery comes the readiness to surrender oneself to the richness of the revelation and the many different forms in which it may come to people. In Stage 5 thinking the celebration of the sacraments, the hearing of the gospel stories, and participation in liturgy become more than routine rituals.

Stage 5 persons are open to the possibility that symbols can communicate in ways that are deeper and more powerful than the most sophisticated descriptive concepts and propositions. Such persons are also aware of the depths of knowing something within themselves.

Faith-knowing, which at Stage 4 is chiefly intellectual, becomes open to a felt sense of the world and God, a knowing which can be apprehended only at deeper levels of awareness than reasoning provides. This does not mean a sacrifice of the gains of Stage 4 reasoning, but rather a personal expansion and deepening of knowing beyond anything yet attained.

Returning to the analogy of a mapmaker, imagine an encounter between two Stage 5 persons who have mapped the territory of faith experiences. As distinguished from a person at Stage 4, they will be ready to compare their maps without prejudgments, will make corrections where these seem warranted, and may even withhold final judgment where there seem to be irreconcilable differences between the maps.

At Stage 5 the believer is ready for dialogue with others who also have deeply felt convictions about what they believe. A Stage 4 encounter of this type would result in an argument or debate, each person becoming more convinced that his or her viewpoint is the only correct one. At Stage 5 there is interchange, even openness to conversion, and at least some learning of new ways to look at things.

This stage calls for understanding, literally "standing under" where the other person is standing, and seeing the world from that vantage point. Only the person who has confidence in his or her own positions of faith will be able to engage in such dialogue freely and openly. Such is the believer at Stage 5.

Stage 6. "I have a dream."

These words of Martin Luther King Jr. are from his famous speech delivered at the peak of the civil-rights movement. They captured the imagination of a nation which had come to recognize the evils of racial discrimination.

These words of Martin Luther King Jr. would not have been as powerful if King had not become a living symbol of the dream that he invited others to share. It was a dream of unity, of a time when people of different color and creed would live together in peace and harmony. It was a dream of justice and equal opportunity for all people. It was a dream of love, a vision of a common humanity linked by mutual respect and care.

Faith development to this stage of thinking is exceedingly rare. The few perons who reach it have, in the words of Jesus, lost their lives for the sake of the gospel (Mark 8:35). In so doing they have found a new meaning for their lives in God and in relation to all humanity.

Persons at Stage 5 still find it necessary to preserve their partial visions, even though they have been captivated by the dream of a larger, more inclusive reality that Jesus called the kingdom of God. The person at Stage 6 is living *in* the dream, which is not yet a reality but a movement toward and a partial realization of it. The strength of a person who has reached this stage is the ability to surrender to this dream, however limited its actual fulfillment might be.

Candidates for Stage 6 do not have to be great leaders who have changed the history of the world or great saints who have become well known for their works of mercy, like Mother Teresa of Calcutta. I would suspect that all of us have known someone whom we would nominate as a

Stage 6 candidate. Such persons may be seriously flawed in some dimension of their humanity, but they nonetheless have a special grace that makes them seem like a living representation of the God who is always working at transforming and unifying the world.

But we must keep in mind that the persons functioning in Stage 6 ways may often regress to Stage 5, 4, or 3 ways of thinking and acting. This is most likely to happen when Stage 6 people are confronted by situations they cannot handle. It is then that they may even turn completely to their basic Stage 1 trust in God and complete dependence on him.

Concluding comment

The developmental process we have been tracing through six stages is a movement toward greater comprehensiveness, flexibility, and complexity of faith. Each stage is an advance over the previous stage. Are we to say, then, that Stage 6 is better than Stage 4? The answer to that is both yes and no, depending on how one defines the word *better.*

If by better we mean higher achievement or greater value, then the answer must be no. Every person is a totally and unconditionally loved child of God regardless of accomplishments, of resolution of life-cycle crises, or of the level of faith-knowing. But if by better we mean a more mature, more self-fulfilled stage, then the answer is yes.

That yes, however, is no reason for pride any more than being at Stage 2 is cause for despair. As any Stage 6 person will tell you, growing in faith is a gift rather than an accomplishment, grace rather than self-achievement. Stage 6 people are actualizations of the promise that we all are invited to share in Jesus Christ, "according to the grace given to us" (Romans 12:6).

Reflecting on faith as trust

Try to imagine the day of your Baptism. If you were baptized as an infant, think of yourself as a baby being held securely in the arms of your mother or father or one of your godparents. If you were baptized at a later age, think of the pastor laying the hand of blessing on your head.

Now hear the promise that accompanies the action: You are baptized. Nothing can separate you from the love of God in Christ Jesus—not the evil that is in the very fabric of human existence, not your frailties or your failures, not the shadow of death that grows darker as the years go by. Through all of your life the arms of a loving God will enfold you because God is your heavenly mother and father, and you are one of his children.

Next, turn your thoughts to some of the scary things that have happened to you. What is the most frightening thing you can remember? How old were you at the time? Picture in your mind the place where it happened. What made it so frightening to you?

Now try to recall how you dealt with your fear. What enabled you to make it through that frightening experience? What was your source of security amidst the danger? Was the person or thing you trusted trustworthy? Did you experience God's presence or did he seem far away?

Finally, take a moment to bring together these two images—the image of your Baptism and the image of your most frightening experience. Imagine having the loving arms of God around you where you are reliving your most frightening experience. What is your experience as these images merge?

In thee our fathers trusted; they trusted, and thou didst deliver them.

Psalm 22:4

Chapter Four
TRUST:
THE FUNDAMENTAL
ORIENTATION
OF FAITH

The capacity to trust is very important to our humanity. We could not begin to become independent, autonomous persons if it were not possible for us to trust ourselves, others, and the world in which we live. Most of the time we take the need to trust for granted, like, for example, the need to believe that the people on whom we depend will not desert us.

Little children do not take trust for granted in the same way adults can. Infants are not born with the confidence that they live in a safe and secure world. When a parent leaves, a young child often panics and cries. Relief is apparent when the parent returns. Only a safe environment, symbolized by a protecting and caring mother or father, makes it possible for an infant to develop the kind of trusting attitude that will enable it to face life unafraid.

A parent develops a sense of trust in a child by a relationship that combines sensitive care of the child's needs with a sense of a parent's trust-worthiness. Such trust is certainly not a rational judgment. It is more of a felt response to a total environment.

The universal experience of trust-mistrust

We human beings all fail to trust some people and some things (often with good reason). In some respects we ought not trust even God (as, for example, in the case of our tempting him with a foolish action). But it is doubtful that a person can live without some measure of trust.

Furthermore, trust and mistrust usually exist side by side and in tension with each other. The developmental problem related to this tension is learning how to deal with the tension.

Infants who lack a sense of trust are the best evidence we have of the need for a parental environment that creates trust. A number of studies were made of children who were institutionalized during the first year of their life. The physical needs of such children were fully met, including medical care superior to what they would have received in a home. They lacked only the tender nurturing care of a mother or father. But in that "only" lay the difference between life and death, because 50 percent of such children who lacked tender loving car died within the first year of life. Most of the others later bore marks of severe psychological damage.

The negative counterpart to trust is mistrust, both being common to the experience of every child. Together they form the base of the conflict that dominates the first developmental stage of human life.

It would be neither possible nor healthy to raise a child in an environment in which there was no occasion whatever for mistrust. Such a child would be poorly prepared for a world in which an appropriate measure of mistrust is a necessity for survival. But the conflict between trust and mistrust needs a resolution that allows the child to have a basically trusting attitude toward life. This resolution of the tension makes the child ready to move into the next developmental stage.

How can a parent convey to a child the feeling that its needs will be provided? A parent can be a source of security for the child only if she or he is a basically secure person. And the parent can be secure only if she or he has a source of security.

A parent who cannot trust is unable to call forth trust in a child. Adults must therefore gain from others and from their religion a fund of assurance that enables them to meet the needs of the next generation.

The religious roots of trusting

In Erikson's view every person needs religion or something very nearly like it in order to survive psychologically, for religion is the systematic undergirding of basic trust for all of life.

Erikson is interested in the psychological function of religion, not its truth. The question he asks of any religion is whether or not it is able to accomplish that systematic reassurance that a parent must give if a young child is to have basic trust. If it does, then for Erikson that religion is psychologically sound, assuming that it is not at the same time undermining other basic human needs, for example, the need for autonomy.

Erikson also observed that most people cannot afford to be without religion. Take the case of a child who wakes up in the night and finds itself surrounded by darkness, beset by nameless threats, and alone. In the terror of the moment the child cries out for its mother or father, who comes and embraces the child and whispers, "Don't be afraid; everything is all right." The parent's assurance is a lie apart from a religious interpretation of human existence. The trust a parent proffers to the child must be undergirded by a trustworthy universe.

Martin Luther noted the religious roots of trusting when he said that no one lives without faith, without trusting something or someone. "A god is that to which we look for all good and in which we find refuge in every time of need. To have a god is nothing else than to trust and believe him with our whole heart. As I have often said, the trust and faith of the heart alone make both God and an idol. If your faith and trust are right, then your God is the true God. On the other hand, if your trust is false and wrong, then you have not the true God. For these two belong together, faith and God. That to which your heart clings and entrusts itself is, I say, really your God."[5]

Even in this passage Luther moves very quickly beyond a commentary on the religious roots of trusting to a theological analysis of the object of one's trust: Is it God or an idol? However, he and Erikson agree that there is always a religious dimension to trust.

What does God promise?

Let us turn now from an analysis of the universal experience of trust, including its religious roots, to an examination of the nature of promise, since it is promise that elicits trust. Our attention will focus on the ultimate kind of promise, namely, the promise of God.

The promise of God is the promise of his presence, a promise that can be traced to the very beginning of creation. More particularly, it is the promise of order, of providence, and of acceptance—each of which will be examined in some detail in the following sections.

God's promises of order, providence, and acceptance are intended for every child at birth. They can be taken for granted. The ground for these promises is the Father of our Lord Jesus Christ. They are promises that come with creation and life. They are intended for every person in every corner of the world.

To withhold or distort the promise or promises of God, for whatever reason, is sin. Sin results in a disordered world that cries for the restoration of divine promise. That restoration takes place in the life, death, and resurrection of Jesus Christ. In him the promise of God's eternal presence and saving power is made certain and overcomes the threat of sin or any conceivable danger.

"I am sure that neither death, nor life, . . . nor anything else in all creation, will be able to separate us from the love of God in Christ Jesus our Lord" (Romans 8:38, 39). That was the faith the apostle Paul had. It was a certain faith based on the promises God gives through his Son, Jesus Christ.

The promise of order

Now let us look more closely at the tension which exists between promise and threat at every level of God's created order, that is, between the promise of order and the threat of chaos.

Sometimes chaos is clearly destructive, as in disease, disintegration, disorder, and ultimately death. These four dreaded d's strike terror into the human soul. In the face of such threats we trust anything that promises to give life and order in the form of integration, health, and wholeness. The greater the promise, the more it is counted on to deliver on its promises.

This is the way faith works: It looks for and responds to the greatest ordering force and puts its trust in that power. Our faith in modern medicine is a good example. Miracle drugs and new cures stir hope that all disease can be eliminated, even to the point that some people are willing to freeze their ravaged bodies in anticipation of a future cure.

Because chaos, wearing the mask of death, eventually wins its battle, faith must rely on a promise of order, a promise more powerful than the most destructive threat of chaos, namely death. Faith discovers such a promise in the person Jesus Christ, who not only heals the sick but ushers in a kingdom from which death has been banished.

Not all chaos stands in such stark opposition to the order that God intended for his creation. Moving through the orderly stages of development would not be healthy or even possible without facing periods of disorganization and tension. Erikson's theory of development assumes an element of conflict that intensifies to the point of crisis at the end of each stage. In the periods of transition there needs to be an underlying assurance that all is in order, that love and life are secure, that everything will be all right.

The promise of providence

The promise of providence is countered by the human terror of powerlessness. We are most powerless in the early years of life when we are totally dependent on the care of parents and others. But not only then. Throughout life we are surrounded by powers over which we have only limited control. So we search out centers of power with which to align ourselves.

Such centers of power are a threat as well as a promise because they cannot always be trusted to act in our best interest. The temptation is to center more and more power in ourselves so that we might become self-sufficient and able to protect ourselves from that which threatens us.

The promise of God is the promise of him who is *the* foundation of power, whether we acknowledge it or not, a God who promises to make life safe for us. The promise does not mean that everything will go smoothly, that if we pray hard enough or believe strongly enough the forces of evil will lose their strength. Such a belief is the error of faith healers and those who promise success as a reward of faith. The promise of God is that "the everlasting arms" are always underneath us and that we will be held securely no matter how great the power that threatens us.

The promise of acceptance

The promise of forgiveness, in tension with the threat of judgment, is the promise of God's unconditional acceptance of us in spite of the worst that we can do to ourselves and others. The term *acceptance* puts us in touch with our earliest experiences of being held, fed, and protected by a loving parent.

If the holding and feeding are good and secure, there is almost nothing that the infant can do that will threaten that relationship and life. Not a biting of the nipple. Not angry flaying of arms and legs. Not even screaming in church. Ordinarily there is little danger that a parent will throw the child down and say, "I'll pick you up only when you stop crying."

This deeply experienced acceptance is what enables a child later to understand a God who can forgive instead of punish, a God who can love when angry, and one who promises a relationship that will never be broken.

The promise of God needs to be heard from the very beginning of life. It is a promise already given in Baptism and mediated daily through the care of loving parents. It does not need to be spoken to be heard any more than rejection needs to be verbalized in order to be felt. *Faith does not await the rise into consciousness and the capacity to "know" any more than does sin.* Promise establishes the foundations of human existence, and the source of such promise is God.

To receive the kingdom of God as a little child, as Jesus said we must, is to be aware of the irrevocable nature of the promises of a loving, caring presence. In the preceding paragraphs I have tried to evoke the earliest awareness that we have of God's presence as it is felt in the promises of order, providence, and acceptance. The roots of faith are embedded in these promises that are heard and felt very early in life.

While faith is felt before it is known, it grows and matures in knowledge and in behavior. The rest of this book is devoted to a study of that process. But the power is in the roots, for in the early years of human life we have the strongest affirmation of promise.

The beginnings of faith

The promises of God not only sustain faith but give it birth. The only way to talk about faith in its beginning is in terms of a receiving of gifts of God and a trusting in his promises.

The beginning is followed by a becoming, a growing which has its roots in promise. But at the beginning of faith there is only promise and the trust that holds on to the promise, a trust that we are and will always remain children of God.

Trust is the assurance that the "giver of all good gifts" will be faithful to his promise of continual love and care. Even as trust is the foundation of human personality, born out of the earliest encounters of parents and child, so also is trust the foundation of faith, born out of the earliest encounter of child and God.

It is exactly the language of trust, born in the act of receiving the gifts of God, that seems most appropriate for talking about faith. A theology that has its focus on the rich and overflowing grace of God will also have a trusting self as the receiver of that grace.

It would be hard to overemphasize the total human dependency on God for faith. This healthy dependency, which is so marked at faith's beginning, remains throughout its lifetime and undergirds its development.

In its beginning faith is essentially passive. If you were to ask what faith does at the beginning stage, the answer would be that it receives the gift of God; it holds on to the promises that are given. The entire initiative is from the divine side; the human response can be described only in terms of receptivity.

The movement is always from God to us, from promise to trust, from gift to reception. "In this is love, not that we loved God but that he loved us and sent his Son to be the expiation for our sins" (1 John 4:10).

The receptive character of faith

Martin Luther put heavy stress on the receptive character of Christian faith. He did so because he knew the human tendency to choose life under law rather than life under the gospel and the consequent need to achieve salvation through hard work and merit.

Luther was so suspicious about having faith in works that he said it is better to keep your eyes focused on the promises of God and forget about experiences. He emphasized that the person who receives "the righteousness of God" is altogether empty of any righteousness and merit.

With such a strong affirmation of the grace of God comes the risk of neglecting the human side of faith. Though both pride and despair can be fostered by constantly examining one's spiritual pulse, it is nevertheless true that faith can be enriched through reflection on experiences as a child of God.

Even in its receiving aspect, faith is an experience. That experience is trust, and we are devoting this entire chapter to what trust in the promises of God means. We shall do the same with other dimensions of faith in the sections that follow. Such reflection does not negate the grace of God. It celebrates the presence of God's grace in our lives and encourages us to find ways to facilitate its growth.

The relational aspect of faith

All of our talk about the human side of faith needs to take place within an understanding of faith as relational. One can make distinctions between the human side of faith (trust) and the divine side of faith (promise) only with the realization that such a distinction is within a relationship.

To speak of God's action independent of a relationship to him is to speak about what we cannot know, since we know him only through faith. To talk about a person with independent powers to receive grace is equally meaningless because a child of God is literally born in the act of faith, literally called into being by the grace of God.

The analogy for a relational understanding of faith is the parent-child relationship. The first response of the child to its mother or father is trust, and that response is literally called into being by the love (the grace) of the parent.

In this analogy of the parent-child relationship, the child does not claim credit for bringing something to the relationship, such as merit, power, or some quality of being (like knowledge or assent). At the same time trust is the response of the child rather than the creation of the parent.

Can you imagine a parent saying to the infant in her or his arms, "I want you to know I can be trusted. I'm a very trustworthy person. I promise to take good care of you. Please believe me!" All these assertions are implicit in the loving care she or he provides, and the child will come to "know" them as true as it gains the capacity to reflect on experience.

Note well the sequence in faith development: *Trust precedes knowledge and assent rather than the other way around.* At the beginning of human growth and faith, trust is a passive-dependent response to the gifts of loving care and the firm promise of more to come. The initiative belongs totally to God, who calls forth the response of trust.

Infant Baptism—infant faith?

An understanding of faith that has its beginnings in the trusting of a God of promise is nowhere more clearly evident than in infant Baptism. Meanings are conveyed more richly where action and word are joined.

The rite of infant Baptism conveys through action and word what we have been trying to say. In Baptism faith is the gift of God through the community (church), even as trust is the gift of the parent to the child. Through Baptism the child is received into relationship with God and the church, even before there is anything that resembles conscious awareness in the child.

Furthermore, infants come to realize the gifts that are already theirs as children of God when the community of faith really means its Baptism. Through Baptism children are literally called by God into relationship with him and are placed into a community of concerned people who have the responsibility of providing settings in which the "becoming of faith" can take place.

Children do nothing to earn their Baptism, their right to be part of the people of God. Later they become aware of who they are: children of God within the community of the faithful. The language of the community, which is the language of faith, becomes familiar and understandable to them while they are growing up as trusting members of the community.

There is no need to ascribe some kind of knowledge or assent of the will to baptized infants. To do so discredits the practice of infant Baptism. In relation to God, the person acknowledges total dependence on the grace of God without eliminating the subject's involvement in the process of receiving that grace. A relational view of human development provides a helpful psychological base for such an understanding of Christian faith.

Lutherans always have maintained that faith is necessary for receiving God's grace in Baptism. The "Apology of the Augsburg Confession" makes that position crystal clear: "We teach that in using the sacraments there must be a faith which believes these promises and accepts that which is promised and offered in the sacrament. The reason for this is clear and well founded. A promise is useless unless faith accepts it."[6] Faith is important—not to make Baptism valid (that depends on the word of command and promise), but to receive the promise.

Although all the early reformers agreed that faith is the receiving hand in Baptism, there were some (later called Baptists) who said that a person can have faith only when he or she is capable of knowing, assenting, and trusting—the three parts of a traditional definition of faith.

Obviously infants do not have the capacity to hear the word of promise spoken at their Baptism and thus cannot grasp them intellectually. So it seems logical to postpone Baptism until children are "of age" and ready to respond with faith to what God promises and does through Baptism.

While favoring the strong emphasis on faith in Baptist tradition, Lutherans rejected the idea of postponing Baptism. In so doing, they followed Luther's insistence that infants have faith. It was not an easy position to defend since the definiton of faith agreed upon by all sides assumed a capacity for knowing which an infant obviously does not have. Luther simply maintained that infants *do* believe even though he granted that we do not know *how* they believe.

A continuation of the practice of infant Baptism does not rest upon our ability to provide evidence for the presence of faith in infants, but the developmental psychology I am proposing does help make more sense out of the beginnings of faith. Faith has its roots in promise, and trust is the form of this faith as it grasps and clings to the promise.

Faith seeking understanding

Christian theology has always struggled with the problem of relating faith and reason. The phrase "faith seeking understanding" was one of the earliest attempts to suggest the relationship.

According to this formulation, faith precedes reason but depends on reason for both explanation and application. I think that faith and reason are much more closely intertwined than this formulation suggests, especially in later developmental stages. But the phrase indicates that trusting relates to knowing.

In the previous chapter, I provided a synopsis of James Fowler's stages of faith-knowing. In the remainder of this chapter I shall indicate the different forms that trust might take in each of the stages of faith. I will do this on the basis of the story of Abraham's "sacrifice" of Isaac as recorded in Genesis 22.

You may want to read that account in full at this time. In it we told that Abraham was commanded by God to sacrifice Isaac, his dearly loved son of promise. Abraham made all the necessary arrangements and traveled with his son to the appointed place. There he bound Isaac, placed him upon an altar he built, and raised his knife to slay him. Only then did the angel of the Lord call a halt and provide a ram to be offered as a sacrifice instead of Isaac.

This is one of the master stories of trust in the Bible. How might it be interpreted at each of the stages of believing?

Stage 1. "God's just like my mommy and daddy."

Though the preschool child is not likely to catch the story line of the entire narrative, one can anticipate that some of the images are likely to be powerful and easily elaborated by the child's imagination.

The image of a father who can save you or kill you can be very real to a young child. It graphically captures the trust-mistrust conflict of which Erikson speaks. Daddies are big and powerful, and who knows what they might do when they get angry.

Since a child at this stage is likely to identify God with powerful parent figures, the story is likely to be heard in these terms. Not only a young child, but also an adult who is feeling little and powerless may think of God as one who kills and brings to life. So in the mind of a person at this first stage there is no sharp line of differentiation between Abraham (father) and God (Father) and no telling what they might do, depending upon our behavior and their whims.

The story ends with a more powerful image of saving than killing, and hopefully this will match the child's experience of more trust than distrust. But the wisdom of telling this story to a preschool child is questionable because the story is likely to be totally misinterpreted.

Stage 2. "What's fair is fair!"

At this stage we can expect that the story will be taken quite literally and interpreted in terms of the principle of reciprocity, namely, that Abraham got what he deserved. He obeyed God when God told him to take Isaac to a place where Isaac was to be sacrificed on an altar. And Abraham would have slain Isaac if the angel had not stopped him. So God rewarded Abraham for his obedience by providing the ram for a sacrifice.

On the other hand, if Abraham had *disobeyed* God, he would have deserved the punishment he undoubtedly would have received. What kind of punishment? Well maybe he would have lost his son and the promise of

God's blessing in some other way, because God only blesses those who are good and who do what he says.

You can always count on God to be fair, just as he was in this story. That's why you need to obey the Ten Commandments and do the will of God all the time. So goes the reasoning.

Persons at the Stage 2 level of faith are capable of following the story from beginning to end and getting its point, but they are not able to step out of the story and reflect on its meaning. Add to that the strongly anthropomorphic images of God that are characteristic of this period, and the result may be that God is pictured as a stern lawgiver who makes impossible demands that must be obeyed no matter how wrong those commands might seem.

Caught within the story, a Stage 2 person finds no way to understand its meaning other than in the literal way. One only has to think of the blind obedience given to Hitler and Jim Jones to realize the distorted and harmful ways that Stage 2 persons might think about God and themselves in relation to this story.

Stage 3. "I believe what the church believes."

A person at Stage 3 is likely to hear and interpret the story as it is presented in Sunday school, Bible class, Confirmation instruction, and sermons. No longer trapped within the narrative and its literal interpretation, it will be possible to reflect on the meaning of the story in relation to what one learns from other stories and teachings of the church.

However, the person at this stage of faith will not be able to rise above the interpretation given to the story by whatever authority figure is significant in the person's life. For the most part this authority will be the church in the person of its pastor or teachers. The danger for persons at this stage lies in the distorted or inadequate interpretations the church might give to the story and its meaning.

Let me suggest how a Lutheran teacher might interpret this story in the light of law-gospel understanding. The teacher would explain that if the God of Abraham were only a God of law, then the story would be terrifying indeed. It would mean that everyone would have to obey his every command, even the unreasonable one, just as Abraham did, or face the consequences of God's anger and punishment.

However, we know that the God of Abraham is also the God of promise who loved both Abraham and Isaac as his chosen children. We know this from the stories about Abraham, but we know it even more clearly from the story of Jesus Christ.

Abraham trusted in this God of love and promise. He believed that this trust would not be betrayed. It was Abraham's faith in the God of promise and not his strict obedience that God reckoned as righteousness (Romans 4:9).

This is the way the story could be taught and so it would be believed without question by the Stage 3 persons in the congregation.

Stage 4. "As I see it, God is . . ."

Persons at Stage 4 (which is unlikely to be attained in childhood) can be expected to examine this story critically for what it says about the way life is to be lived and how God acts in the world. For individuals no longer satisfied with the conventional wisdom of the church, the story must produce meaning that is rational.

The moral reasoning of this stage would see the need for a world governed by a lawful order with reasonable standards for social roles. A Stage 4 person might ask, "What kind of world would it be if fathers felt directed by

God to kill their sons?" Such a person might reason that a command to kill a son might be disobeyed in the name of maintaining lawful order in the world because only where there is lawful order can people trust one another.

On the other hand, a Stage 4 person might reason that Abraham was right in obeying the command since God is the source of all law and order. He who originally forbade killing can command it since he is the one who ultimately determines the order of things.

A few persons at Stage 4 might go beyond that level of moral reasoning and interpret the story in the light of a universal ethical principle like "the sanctity of life." On the basis of such a principle, it might be argued that Abraham not only had the right but the duty to disobey God's command to kill Isaac. Since the principle that human life is sacred is both absolute and universal, Abraham might have called God to account for what appears to be a fault in the moral order of the universe.

Whichever way the argument might go, I hope the reader will catch the flavor of the critical reflection and the underlying trust in human reasoning that a Stage 4 person might use in understanding the narrative.

A person at Stage 4 will work hard on mapping out the meanings in the Abraham narrative. A critical analysis of ethical issues will be made and may result in a defense of Abraham's moral judgment: his suspension of the strong prohibition against murder in the name of a higher ethical principle.

Stage 5. "Don't confuse the map with the territory."

In a Stage 5 kind of faith a person approaches the story with a desire to see and hear its hidden depths. Concern for a clear statement of meaning fades into the background.

What really happened between Abraham and God in this story? What did God want from Abraham? Was it blind obedience? Was it disciplined moral reasoning? Was it what Kierkegaard called "a leap of faith," by which he meant a suspension of the ethical in response to a divine call to faith? What is the deeper meaning in this master story, the truth that can guide us in our faith struggles? These are the kinds of question a Stage 5 faith might ask.

Luther has provided us with a Stage 5 interpretation of this narrative. He saw in the story a symbol of the Resurrection. Luther placed this thought in the mind of Abraham: "I am reducing my son to ashes. Nevertheless, he is not dying. Indeed, those ashes will be the heir."[7]

How can Isaac be both dead and the heir who will have children through whom the whole world will be blessed? Because God has promised it and because faith holds on to that promise even in the face of evidence that totally contradicts it. So reasoned Luther.

Luther put the same statement of faith into the mouth of Isaac: "God will not lie. I am the son of the promise. Therefore I must beget children, even if heaven collapses."[8]

Nothing less than the structure of the universe is at stake here, according to Stage 5 type of thinking. Take away the promise and everything collapses. Better yet, even if the structure of the universe collapses, the promise of God is still certain.

So it is—Luther went on to say—with our own death. How can one possibly believe that death is not death but life? If we listen to the law, it will tell us that in the midst of life we are in death. The gospel, however, inverts the statement and says that in the midst of death we are in life.

So says St. Paul in 2 Corinthians 6:9: "As dying, and behold we live." On this Luther commented: "This is the power of faith, which mediates in this way between death and life, and changes death into life and immortality, which, as faith knows, has been bestowed through Christ."[9] Through the analogy of faith Luther used the powerful symbol of death and resurrection to reconcile what appears to be the irreconcilable opposites of death and life in the story of Abraham and Isaac.

Not everyone would be able to grasp the meaning of the story at this level of faith-thinking. More than an intellectual grasp of paradox is called for. Needed also is the experience to sense what it might be like for a parent even to consider the killing of his or her dearly loved child. Perhaps then one might have the capacity to "know" in a limited way what Abraham was called to do and what God actually did.

As for me, I see this meaning of the story from afar and stand in wonder of it. But I cannot put myself deeply enough into the story of Abraham and Isaac to grasp its meaning at a level required for Stage 5 faith-thinking.

Stage 6. "I have a dream."

Perhaps at Stage 6 there might be what Kierkegaard called a "knight of faith" who would be capable of identifying with Abraham's willingness to sacrifice everything that was dear to him for the realization of a good that was not at all obvious. But such a person would be hard to find. I have met no one whom I could suggest as a candidate for the role of Abraham. It may be easier to speak of Abraham's experience as a dream, a dream of what it might mean to live totally by promise.

In Chapter 2 I suggested Martin Luther King Jr. as a candidate for Stage 6. But he had the full weight of moral authority behind his actions, even though what he did made him unpopular and eventually cost him his life. Contemporary candidates for Abraham's role are not likely to be well-known figures, since Abraham was required to act in the privacy of his individual conscience.

However, we do have the figure of Jesus as a Stage 6 example, although it would be more accurate to say that Jesus was in the role of a willing Isaac. He knowingly offered his life as a sacrifice at a point in history and in his own life when the future of the promise of God seemed anything but sure. Feeling forsaken by his father and yet crying out "My God," Jesus held on to God's promise even when his dying appeared to be a contradiction of that promise.

Dying, and behold he lives! Thus Jesus became the symbol that Luther used to interpret the story of Abraham and Isaac for Christian faith.

Concluding comment

This exercise of interpreting the meaning of trust in the story of Abraham and Isaac from the perspective of the various stages of faith-knowing has been purely speculative. Using what we know about the characteristics of people at Fowler's six stages of faith, I have illustrated how they *might* hear and interpret this narrative. My purpose was not to validate Fowler's theory of faith stages. It was simply to suggest how it could be used in teaching the great faith stories of the Bible.

Reflecting on your journey of faith

 The journey of faith can be long and varied. Whether you have just recently begun this journey or are well traveled, take a little time to retrace your steps and note some of the changes that have taken place in your faith along the way.

How would you describe your faith during your childhood? Was Confirmation an important event in your life or just something you allowed because your parents wanted you to be confirmed? What happened to your faith during your high school and college years? Did your faith grow, or did you find yourself caring less about church worship, private prayer, ways of nourishing your faith, and other activities?

How significant was your faith as you struggled to discover and establish your vocation? If you have reached midlife, try to see some differences between your faith now and at the time you were confirmed. Would you describe your faith as stronger or weaker, more or less influential in your life? If you have reached later adulthood, compare your faith now with what it was in midlife.

Next, select one particular crisis in your journey of faith. Try to remember as much as you can about this crucial time in your life: the circumstances, the significant relationships, the fundamental issues. How was the crisis resolved? What part did your Christian faith play in the resolution? Was your faith strengthened by your experience or weakened? What did you learn about yourself and your faith that might help in facing future crises?

Let us run with perseverance the race that is set before us, looking to Jesus, the pioneer and perfecter of our faith.

Hebrews 12:1–2

Chapter Five
FAITH DEVELOPMENT IN YOUTH AND ADULTHOOD

Chapters 2 and 3 provide a broad overview of faith formation in terms of life-cycle stages (Erikson) and maturation
patterns (Fowler). In Chapter 4 the earliest stage of the life
cycle was examined more thoroughly for a deeper understanding of the fundamental importance of trust in faith
formation. The structural patterns of faith-seeking-under-
standing were used to explore how the trusting element
of faith might be known or understood at each of the
stages that Fowler has identified.

In this fifth chapter we examine three more stages of
the human life cycle. Each of these is also a stage in the
journey of faith.

The first of these three stages is Erikson's identity versus identity-diffusion crisis, which is a transition period
between childhood and adulthood. Faith formation during this period is a matter of responding to God's "call"
in such a way that I come to know who I am and where I
am going.

The second stage is Erikson's generativity versus
stagnation crisis, which is an extended period of adulthood
from the thirties through the sixties. Faith formation during this period is a matter of fulfilling one's vocation
through caring about others.

The third stage is Erikson's integrity versus despair crisis, the period of late adulthood when faith formation is a matter of surrendering one's life to God who is its author.

Fowler's theory of faith patterns will be applied to each of the above stages of faith formation as in Chapter 4. The faith by which we live in each stage of life seeks understanding. The form our thinking takes is our pattern or stage of faith-thinking.

Between childhood and adulthood

There is no doubt that the movement from childhood to adulthood is a key developmental juncture in the human life cycle. From about age 13 to 30 a young person has the formidable task of becoming captain of his or her own ship. If the child has wise parents, that development will happen gradually as the young person assumes more and more responsibility for decisions that will shape his or her destiny.

Taking charge of one's own life would be a stern test of inner strength even if the seas were calm, but the transition between childhood and adulthood is potentially the stormiest and most chaotic period in a person's entire life.

In this transition in which so many changes take place, the identity question must be faced head on: "Who am I?" and "Where am I going?" A young person will not be able to chart a clear course on the sea of life unless he or she has formulated some answers to those basic questions.

It is not that a child lacks a sense of identity prior to adolescence. The earliest sense of who I am goes all the way back to the mirror of the parent's smiling face by which is gained a primal sense of the goodness of being and growing. With adequate parenting a child will experience the gradual unfolding of a self that can integrate a variety of experiences into a sense of being the same "me."

I am the person who eats with a knife and fork, goes to church on Sunday, plays ball, prays, goes to bed every night, and gets up every morning. In a relatively healthy person there is a feeling of sameness about the "I" who does all these things. However, there could be considerable confusion if, for instance, a child is forced to live in two worlds that call for two different identities. This can happen when a child of divorced parents lives with mother during the week and father on weekends or vice versa.

In any case the developing self-identity of a child is more gift than choice. Parents and other adults make all the early decisions about what their children will be and the ways they should go.

Those decisions are more far-reaching than any of us realize on a conscious level. In the home, community, and society at large most adult decisions are taken for granted as fully appropriate. They involve such matters as wearing clothes, using the toilet, going to school, being polite, and eating.

Beyond decision making, the parent's own behavior shapes the identity of their children in unconscious ways—as when parents play classical music, smoke cigarettes, or hug each other. Few parents (and teachers) pay attention to the significance of their everyday behavior in the forming of childrens' ideas until something happens that reveals how powerful an influence adults are in the lives of children.

Effective parenting of youth

Effective parenting maintains concern for the destiny of the child without squelching the emerging autonomy of the "I." Youth need a structured environment within which they have a clear sense of who they are and what is expected of them.

Youth who are not blessed with such an environment may develop fragile identities that easily crumble under stress. For a strong identity it is usually better to have too much structure than too little, though some individuals develop greater strength because they are left to their own self-determination.

The same principle holds for the shaping of a *Christian* identity. All of the early decisions that are so crucial to a sense of who I am as a child of God are made by parents. The first and most important decision parents can make is to have their child baptized. In Baptism God speaks the words he spoke at Jesus' baptism: "This is my beloved [child]." In that promise is laid the cornerstone of a Christian's identity.

When Martin Luther was most unsure of himself and his future in the darkest days of his reformation of the church, he would say to himself, "I am baptized." For him the most fundamental fact of his existence was that he had been baptized a child of God and that in Jesus Christ God was his loving, caring father. With that faith at the center of his being, no stormy sea, whether internal or external, could pose any ultimate threat. So it is with us.

Faithful parents continue to shape their baptized children's sense of who they are through their example, through family devotions, through the reading and telling of Bible stories, through teaching prayer, by sending their children to schools of the church, and by taking their children with them to church services and church activities. Although knowledge is basic to assent, so are experiences.

I can never remember a time when I did not feel that I was a part of the family and fellowship of the church, and I thank God and my parents for that. This given identity is important to the way one comes to know the language of faith. A child learns the use of language first as a member of the family. Language helps children to differentiate themselves from others and also to communicate more effectively. Simple words like love and trust are useful when they help children identify their feelings.

The same applies to the language of faith. The simple statement that "God loves you" makes little sense to a child if the love and the presence of God are not experienced within the home. So the language of faith by which children learn to identify themselves as children of God comes first as a gift before they use it to make a statement of personal decision to be a child of God.

The practice of Confirmation

The traditional practice of Confirmation falls heavily on the side of the *giving* of Christian identity rather than a *choosing* of it. By "traditional" I mean Confirmation at age 12, 13, 14, or 15, with one, two, or three years of instruction preceding it. The purpose of this educational process is to provide a framework for the child's identity as a child of God and to "confirm" that identity.

In the past that process of confirmation was heavily intellectual, emphasizing such things as the memorization of Luther's *Small Catechism* and numerous Bible passages. More recently educators have emphasized the nurturing and shaping of the whole person. In either case the goal of Confirmation is to confirm an identity that has already been given.

But a distinction needs to be made between two phases of development alternating back and forth in the life of a growing child. One is a dependence on learnings (the *Catechism*), sources of authority (the pastor), and institutions (the church). The other is a phase characterized by independent action, problem solving, involvement in life, and a general attitude of experimentation.

In the period of Confirmation instruction, there is a sharp reversal from a general pattern of growth toward greater independence and involvement in life. In early adolescence a young person is seeking authoritative information at a time when mental structures are shifting, physical changes are radical, and general self-assurance is low.

Confirming children during early adolescence takes advantage of their high level of dependence on external authority to reinforce a belief system which had been less systematic prior to this point. Through catechetical instruction and Confirmation, the church provides a Christian identity that the young person has not yet chosen.

Faith-thinking at Confirmation

At this point it will be helpful to turn to Fowler's stages of faith in order to gain better insight into the way faith seeks understanding at the time of Confirmation. You will recall that Stage 3 is characterized as a conformist stage in that what one believes is deeply influenced by the expectations and judgments of significant others. The significant others usually are the parents, the church school teachers, and the pastor in the religious life of the child.

As yet the confirmand has not been in a position either to accept or reject the bestowed identity. It has not yet been tested against other life perspectives, nor has it been applied in ambiguous and conflicting life situations. While beliefs and values are deeply felt, they are largely unexamined and will remain so until the person feels the need to step outside them to examine them, a step necessary for personal commitment.

Catechetical instruction climaxing in Confirmation is well suited to Stage 3 faith formation. That is why it works so well and has become such a solid part of church tradition in spite of the fact that there is little theological and no sacramental support for its practice. The custom not only has no sacramental basis. Some liturgical scholars even argue that Confirmation actually detracts from the centrality of Baptism. However, if Confirmation were eliminated, the church would need to invent something else that would work as well as Confirmation for Stage 3 faith formation.

The problem is not so much with the present practice and age of Confirmation as with the deep-seated attitude that Confirmation is the end stage of faith development. Pastors and Christian educators have long bemoaned the fact that Confirmation is more of a graduation than an initiation for most youth of the church, more of an end stage than a significant milestone in an ongoing process of faith development.

That no more changes are to be fostered and expected and that one can and should remain at this stage of faith formation for the rest of his or her life—these assumptions are the root of the negative aspects of Confirmation.

However, we would be ill advised to abandon a practice that is relatively effective in accomplishing what it is intended to do; namely, to facilitate a solid Stage 3 form of faith-knowing that provides a cornerstone for the identity formation of a young person in early adolescence. In Chapter 6 we shall consider some proposals for the nurturing of faith beyond Confirmation. This may help to locate Confirmation within a lifelong process of faith nurture.

When an intellectual framework of meaning is provided through an intensive catechetical program at ages 12 to 14, the concern can shift to the lived meaning of that faith during the high school years. Through all of this, however, Christian identity is more given by the church than chosen by the child. Such an identity can become very secure when undergirded by a strong identification with the church and an integrated set of beliefs. But we must acknowledge that such an identity remains unexamined and largely taken for granted.

Leaving home

Something happens to a young person when he or she leaves home, usually at the end of high school. The person may leave to go to college or to the armed services, to find a job and live more independently in an apartment, or to get married.

The shift initiated by this move is not a shift to a new developmental stage in Erikson's scheme of the human life cycle. Identity formation remains the fundamental task of personality and faith development. But the shift that takes place is a shift away from the familial, communal, and institutional supports of an identity which has been more given than chosen, up to this point.

That shift may be slight or drastic, depending on the individual's readiness for it; but in any case it is likely to bring to the surface a pressing question: "Is the name Christian, Lutheran, Republican, successor-to-my-father's-trade (or business), follower-of-my-mother's-profession, and so on, the name I want to claim for myself?"

Though this question is likely to surface for any young person leaving home, it is almost inevitable for college students. Beliefs, values, and ideals are challenged by books, professors, and other students. There is no longer a single authority or a consensus of authority figures to say what is right and what is wrong, what to believe and value, or how to chart one's course.

This is a painful transition for most young people, and there are few who complete it without a good deal of floundering or a feeling of wandering through a wilderness. The task of the young adult leaving home is to establish a provisional identity. This takes time and is likely to involve some false starts and poor choices, some of them potentially tragic.

The young adult must define the self first of all in relation to his or her given identity. The young adult will either affirm, reject, or, what is most likely, revise that identity. This development begins with a growing apart, which leaving home accomplishes both physically and symbolically. Such separation may precipitate acts which veer from parental beliefs and values, like getting drunk on Saturday night and sleeping in on Sunday morning.

But that intoxicating freedom is accompanied by a new sense of loneliness and responsibility for charting one's own path. The young adult leaving home is fortunate if he or she is not forced into making premature commitments. One of the pluses of a college education is that it allows a young adult four years to find a personal inner base from which to make the critical choices that will shape the future.

This is a difficult period also for those who have given the child an identity and must now wait to see how well it will fit and how long it will wear. Erikson notes that youth have the power to confirm those who confirm them; this they do by their responses and actions, telling the elders whether life represented by the old and presented to them has meaning for them.

Parents, pastors, and educators often speak of a feeling of helplessness during this time, a helplessness that easily turns to despair if the choices young people make are contrary to the ideals cherished by these adults.

Faith becomes a matter of personal choice at this time. A vow of lifetime loyalty or a promise of faithfulness "even unto death" has often been associated with Confirmation. To make such a promise personally and deeply is beyond the capability of a thirteen-year-old, but personal commitment does become appropriate for the young adult who has left home and has begun the task of assuming responsibility for his or her own Christian identity.

If such identity is to be their own, the young adults can and must make a personal decision to accept and value their Christian heritage. This does not happen all at once, and much of it happens below the level of awareness; but it must happen. Although the act of commitment may lack a dramatic moment of decision, it can never be completely automatic.

Transition to Stage 4

Leaving home is often the trigger for a transition from Stage 3 ("I believe what the church believes") to Stage 4 ("As I see it, God is . . ."). This transition rarely happens in less than four years and can take as long as ten years. The transition usually happens through an encounter with people who understand God and his relation to his world in a variety of ways.

The initial response to this encounter may intensify a Stage 3 way of thinking into an us-versus-them mentality. Gradually, however, there is likely to be a growing respect for expressions of faith that may be very different.

This shift in faith is particularly obvious in college students trained to reflect critically on the thoughts and teachings of others. No longer dependent on authorities for right answers to questions of beliefs and values, the young adult begins to know and to trust his or her own perceptions, experiences, and understandings. All this makes possible the development of a genuinely personal faith that is one of the distinguishing marks of a Stage 4 kind of faith.

Commitment to one's own personal faith may have a rather strong "over against" quality in the early stages of this transition. Many parents find their cherished beliefs challenged by college students who can be almost consumed by a passion to analyze and critique everything they have been taught.

Wise parents allow their children to test and trust their own convictions enough to live with inevitable conflicts between what they believe and what others believe. This shift of center from "out there" to "in here" is precarious and often filled with doubts of both God and self, but a successful transition to Stage 4 makes possible a sense of personal responsibility for one's own faith and strong fidelity to it.

Last phase of identity formation

A further phase of identity formation occurs as young adults find their place in adult society. This doesn't happen immediately after a young person leaves home. Some young people enter college; some join the armed services; some become apprentices; some move from job to job in trying to find where they fit. Rarely does a person settle into an adult life structure until the late twenties or early thirties.

Levinson has provided us with a helpful way to think about this process of moving into a clearly defined adult role. He speaks of the formation of a dream in young adulthood.[10] A dream has the quality of a vision of what may come.

At times the vison may be filled with high drama, like winning the Nobel Prize or making a million dollars; while at other times it may be mundane but equally inspiring, like being a good homemaker or skilled craftsman. The young adult has the task of finding ways to make his or her dream happen.

There is a danger that the dream may become one's god, an end in itself. In our competitive society young adults feel a strong need to make a place for themselves and prove their worth. In striving for achievement, the dream can become the substance of faith, the promise which one trusts, and the master to whom one is loyal.

In more explicitly theological language, the temptation is to justify oneself on the basis of personal merit and demonstrated worth. The problem of burn-out, which affects many who are striving hard to climb the ladder of success, is directly related to an all-consuming need to achieve in the world of adults.

To give young adults a dream without their becoming tyrannized by it is one of the great challenges of the Christian faith. People are tyrannized by a dream when its achievement becomes a proof of their self-sufficiency. They are tyrannized by a dream when they look to themselves alone as the source of the dream and as the only ones who can make it come true. They are tyrannized by a dream when they and the dream are one.

Many of the stories in Levinson's study are examples of the tyranny of dreams, a faith in self-sufficiency for building a permanent identity and a promising future.

Covenant life with God

In the Scriptures we are confronted by a different image of ourselves and a different kind of dream life. It is an image of covenant in which God confers upon us a worth that we could never generate on our own. It is an image of a God who desires more good for us than we do for ourselves. Being rooted in that covenant relationship, we are freed from the tyranny of our dreams and can seek their fulfillment in ways that serve to fulfill the dreams of others as well.

A dream set within a covenant becomes a vocation. Vocation means calling. A Christian's calling begins with Baptism. It confers upon people their identity as children of God and calls them to be a people with a purpose. Not just any purpose, of course. Not a self-chosen purpose. In Christian Baptism we are called to be conformed to the image of God's Son, Jesus Christ, and to be agents of his loving purposes (Romans 8:28).

You can trace the purposes of God throughout the history of his covenant relationship with Israel. However, it is in the sending of his Son that we have the purest expression of God's plan and purpose for the world. The baptism of Jesus was his calling to fulfill the purpose of his Father. He fulfilled that calling by eating and drinking with sinners, by healing the sick, by feeding the hungry, by sharing the condition of the poor, by teaching the Word of God, by dying the death of sinners.

Vocation means befriending sinners, making their burden our own, being a blessing to those around us, building the kingdom of God by carrying on the mission of Christ and his church.

For a dream to be a vocation it must be a blessing to others as well as to one's self. As Frederick Niedner has said so well, "Work is vocation when the worker puts himself or herself into the place of the consumer or client, some other sinner who, perhaps, needs the product of the other's labor for his or her own service to still other sinners."[11]

How many young adults conceive of their dreams in such a fashion? Not many, I suppose, because they fear that it would mean giving up on what makes life exciting and satisfying. But no so! As Frederick Buechner said, "The place God calls you to is the place where your deep gladness and the world's deep hunger meet."[12] A dream is a vocation when God's purpose is linked to the choice of a role in life that engenders a deep sense of satisfaction and enjoyment.

Not everyone finds that intersection of gladness and need throughout their lives. Some never find it at all. Still others who are joyfully fulfilling God's purpose remain unrecognized in a world that puts a lot of emphasis on "making it" by achieving some measure of success. The vocation of a bedridden grandmother who has patience and courage to offer as a witness to her faith may remain hidden in the back ward of a nursing home.

But Jesus' identity, too, was hidden to all at the time of his death. And Christ promised that every act of faith in

God's love, no matter how seemingly trivial or obscure, would have its reward.

Need for ongoing support

We have come a long way from Confirmation, that special effort at forming the identity a Christian receives by Baptism. Confirmation is something like the christening of a ship, constructed as soundly as possible, then sent forth with grand ceremony. But the ship must cross a vast and often turbulent sea, where wind and wave test it before it finds safe harbor again. The safe harbor is a secure adult identity within the fellowship of Christ's church.

Most youth get very little help in making the difficult journey of faith after Confirmation, partly because they do not want the help offered, but perhaps also because parents and the church invest less care and effort after a person is confirmed. Some other cultures and religions have more comprehensive rites of passage in which the community is involved in every phase of the individual's movement from childhood to adult life.

We have charted the course of faith's journey in this dangerous period of life, but our youth need more than a map. They need our personal guidance along the way.

The maturing of faith in midlife

It is evident that a major transition takes place in the growth of a person from child to adult. Dramatic physical changes are matched by a major shift from dependence to independence in almost every aspect of life—financially as one gains employment, psychologically as a sense of personal identity emerges, and socially as one establishes a separate place of residence.

Human development at midlife lacks the high drama and the clear before-and-after demarcations of the adolescent period, but a transition clearly takes place. Ask people in their forties. They feel it as their children begin to leave home. They are aware of it when they no longer expect that life's fulfillment lies somewhere in the future (when they will graduate, when they will get that promotion, when things will settle down). They recognize it in the felt need for refreshment and growth. In this period there are subtle shifts rather than radical dislocations.

A time to dream again

In the previous section we spoke of the dream as one of the keystones in the formation of an adult identity, the dream being an image of how a young adult will make a name for himself or herself.

Of course, not every dream comes true. Very few dreams come true in the way they are first imagined. Midlife is the time for a person to look at his or her earlier dream once more and perhaps to dream again.

It may be that the person is so far from the realization of the earlier dream that it is necessary to abandon the dream or to adjust the dream by scaling it down to more realistic proportions.

For a mother whose children are off to college, it may be the time for the awakening of a dream which has long lain dormant. For others it may be the dream of moving from one place to another, of leaving one vocation to go to another.

This process of coming to terms with one's dreams takes time and the capacity for some inner reflection: Does my life have sufficient purpose, meaning, or direction? Do I find satisfaction in what I am doing? Are there opportunities and challenges that I have ignored up until now and could consider?

The Christian dream of a kingdom of heaven is also a vocation, the intersection between one's gladness and the world's need. For many the dream of Christian vocation will receive a more ready hearing at midlife than in early adulthood.

The goals of early adulthood tend to be directed toward success, productivity, and "making it" in the adult world. If the achievement of those goals proves to be a blessing to others, well and good, but that is not where the young adult's motivation and energy come from. At midlife, however, there develops in many persons a concern for the next generation. But this concern for others is only in its budding stage in early adulthood.

What happens at midlife to make the difference? Erikson uses the word *generativity* to account for the mature adult's deepening concern for what a person has produced, be that children or a product of one's labor. In midlife there is a growing capacity to identify with the needs of others and to find personal fulfillment in serving those needs.

Productivity comes to full blossom in generativity. The desire to prove oneself matures into a yearning for self-expression and self-fulfillment. (This in turn matures into a need to be needed by the object one has produced.) Parenthood is the model for such generativity. However, any project that is "my baby" can be the object cared for and a blessing to others.

As human beings mature in Christian faith, such caring extends beyond the boundaries of their little worlds and includes the needy wherever they may be. No longer finding it necessary to center the world around themselves and their success, people in midlife can sustain with some consistency a concern for the well-being of others.

This shift from a centering of life in oneself to the investment of it in others is at the heart of the Christian's call to ministry. And midlife is the time when that call is most likely to be heard and followed.

Christian vocation in midlife

At first I considered introducing the term *vocation* with the midlife transition since there is a greater readiness for its meaning at this time of life. But Christian faith calls for one's dream to be seen as vocation from the very beginning of adult life or even sooner. Although children and youth, too, can respond positively to the idea that their lives are to be a blessing to others, youth lack some of the deeper levels of caring that are possible at midlife.

As young adults move toward and into the midlife period, their idealism needs to be kept alive and challenged so that their caring vocation will mature. No longer needing to look to the future for the realization of their hopes and desires, Christians in the middle years can be the persons they have spent so much time and energy in becoming.

It takes almost forty years for most people to feel settled in a life position where they can use their resources for something more than future security. Some people never reach that stage of feeling settled and secure. But for those who do, the middle years are a grand occasion for rich experiences in Christian living, the fruit of faith.

Midlife crisis

Why then the talk about a crisis at midlife? One of the ironies of human life is that at the very time when an adult realizes more fully the potential of his or her powers, there comes a corresponding awareness of the limits of those powers. After age forty the physical evidence of some aging becomes too obvious to be denied, especially when it is seen in the faces and figures of classmates at a high school or college reunion.

But it is not just physical limits that must be faced. It is the gradual dissolution of a vibrant family life as the children begin to leave home. It is the feeling that no more promotions are likely to be coming one's way. It is being aware that there are more yesterdays than tomorrows. It is acknowledging that endings are as much a part of life as beginnings.

Learning to live within limits (of accomplishment, of energy, of life itself) is a special gift of faith at midlife. Part of what it means to be human is to be limited. Limitations obviously distinguish humans from God, who is immortal, omnipotent, omniscient.

Knowing our limitations is however a strength rather than a weakness, when viewed from the perspective of Christian faith, because it reminds us that faith's fundamental orientation is trust in God. He promises to care for us better than we can care for ourselves and to sustain us within the limits of our humanity.

Transition to Stage 5

The capacity for reflection which comes with Stage 5 in faith development can deepen and enrich faith through the middle years. One can acknowledge the limits of one's understanding of the mystery of God's revelation at the very times when one is probing the depth of those mysteries.

There is a maturity in reflection that often matches the maturity of caring characteristic of these years. This maturity has more to do with depth and openness than clarity.

A person who has reached a Stage 5 level of faith-knowing in the middle years will be able to benefit from a program of spiritual direction and learning as at no other time of life. Praying, doing the liturgy, reading the Bible, sharing the experiences of faith with others, meeting the needs of others—all these activities of Christian living are avenues for the deepening and broadening of faith particularly in midlife years.

The Stage 5 way of knowing one's faith through participation in activities that cultivate the life of the spirit is characterized by attentiveness to depth and mystery. Such experiences of knowing God with deep personal feeling enliven the journey of faith through the middle years and lessen the fears that come with awareness of human limitations.

Christian faith in late adulthood

Then there comes a time when it is more appropriate to look back than to look forward. Integrity, according to Erikson, is looking back on one's life and its values and affirming them. Only such integrity can balance the despair of feeling finished, helpless (as at the beginning), and hopeless.

Late adulthood can be a time of active involvement in a full and zesty life in which choice rather than duty determines the daily agenda. More and more people maintain healthy and vigorous lives well past the age of retirement. Many of them describe these years as the happiest of their lives. While praising God for the goodness of such blessings, we need to remember that "letting go" is more necessary at this time of life than "taking hold."

For most people the primary symbol of letting go comes at the time of retirement. At retirement I lose the identity that I worked so hard to secure in young adulthood. I am no longer a teacher, or an accountant, or a craftsman, or a plant foreman; I am retired.

Throughout our lives we are taught in countless ways by our society that our worth is determined by our productivity. To let go of this anchor of identity and self-worth requires an act of faith. It also needs the support of a community that affirms the value God places upon human life, not a worth dependent on the amount or quality of work that a person does. Retirement or loss of job at any time of life is one of the greatest tests of our belief that we are justified by grace and not by works.

There are many other ways in which late adulthood becomes a time of letting go. Physical beauty and strength usually wanes noticeably in later years, and it is difficult to accept these changes if our self-worth has been closely identified with an earlier physical image. This problem is especially acute for athletes and movie stars, but it is shared by everyone who looks into the mirror and notices wrinkles, flabby skin, graying hair, and expanding hips and waist.

Then there is the letting go of children who have by now established their own households, often far away. Gradually older people must let go of these and other spheres of power and influence found in institutions and groups. Especially difficult in late adulthood is the letting go of important relationships because of debilitating disease and death of dear friends and relatives. The trip to the funeral home becomes more frequent.

The final release

All of this is preparation for the final letting go that is our own dying. From Erikson's viewpoint, death in late adulthood offers a sense of completion, of fulfillment, to a human life. Having lived a full life, the person in old age can look back with a sense of integrity and fulfillment and can thereby become ready for death with a degree of peace.

But in facing death one needs more than an affirmation of life and its values. Death, from a Christian perspective, is a consequence of sin. Death is not the natural end of a life lived with integrity. It is rather the judgment of God on a life that failed to become what God intended it to be.

The Christian gospel enables a person to face death with hope as well as peace. Hope in the promise of God, "who gives life to the dead and calls into existence the things that do not exist" (Romans 4:17), takes us back from the end of human physical life on earth to the beginning, back to Baptism and the action of a God who brought us from death to life, from sinner to saint.

This God has promised that the life he bestowed in Baptism is a life without ending. Jesus said, "He who believes in me, though he die, yet shall he live, and whoever lives and believes in me shall never die" (John 11: 25–26).

We need to draw heavily on a theology of Baptism at the end of life, reminding each other that the real death of a Christian occurred in the entrance rite of initiation into the church. Endings and beginnings are deeply intertwined in the gracious action of a God who puts an end to the power of sin and death at the very beginning and promises resurrection and new beginnings at the very end.

The promise of resurrection and eternal life, so precious to us as we face endings, is there from the very beginning when we are incorporated through our Baptism into Christ's death and resurrection.

What a marvel that we are from our earliest beginning as Christians wrapped in a love so encompassing that no threat can penetrate it. That is what it means to be baptized, to be held by the loving arms of God like a small infant cradled in the arms of a loving parent.

The promise implicit in such holding is that no harm will come near us. No danger is big enough to undermine the security in this warm embrace. Such a promise is big enough for the surrender called for in our dying.

Reflecting on the feeding of faith

On the left-hand side of a piece of paper jot down a list of experiences in which you felt your faith was nurtured or changed. You needn't take a lot of time for this or be concerned about a chronological sequence. Just write a few words that will identify those experiences that come to your mind; five or six of them will do. Then put the experiences in chronological order on the right side of the paper, select one that stands out as particularly noteworthy, and write a paragraph about that experience.

Questions to consider: Where were you at the time? Who was with you? Was it a group setting or were you alone or with just one or two others? What made it such a meaningful moment in your life? What impression of God surfaces in your mind as you think about that experience?

Next, consider times when you have been in the position of nurturing the faith of others—as a parent, friend, teacher, counselor, pastor. After listing some of these experiences, single out the one you think was especially significant and write a brief paragraph about it. Use the previous questions as recollection starters. Write whatever comes to your mind without trying to organize your thoughts.

Then take a few moments to compare the two experiences you described. Do you nurture the faith of others the way you were nurtured, or have you tried to give to others what was missing in your own faith development? What stands out as most noteworthy in all your memories of nurturing Christian faith in others?

So faith comes from what is heard, and what is heard comes by the preaching of Christ.

Romans 10:17

Chapter Six
THE NURTURING OF FAITH

The nurturing of faith is what the church's educational mission is all about. This chapter will explore faith nurture from a developmental point of view.

A developmental viewpoint is only one way of looking at the question of how faith is fostered, but it is valuable. It provides a basis for determining the needs and capacities of those who receive nurture and also a basis for evaluating the nurture given.

The word *nurture* comes from a Latin term that means to nurse, to suckle, to nourish. It includes the giving of gentle loving care along with nourishment. Educationally the word refers to a fostering of a person's development, hence, to influence, educate, and train.

But the nurturing of faith involves much more than teaching. It is attending to the needs and capacities of persons who are in relationship to God. That calls for human relationships within which faith can be shared and shaped.

This is not to minimize the importance of the intellect in the nurturing of faith. But it underscores that the mind is only one aspect of a process that calls for the participation of the whole person in all aspects of a person's life.

Using developmental insights

What can studies of human development tell us about the nurturing of faith? They cannot tell us how to control the development in a manner that insures the growth of faith, no matter how sophisticated our knowledge of those theories might become. Faith is fundamentally a gift, and the workings of the Spirit of God in the lives of people is a mystery that we shall never be able to comprehend fully, much less control.

"The wind blows where it will, and you hear the sound of it, but you do not know whence it comes or whither it goes; so it is with everyone who is born of the Spirit," Jesus told Nicodemus (John 3:8).

However, God operates in and through nature and history, and so we can expect a pattern in the process of faith formation. And we can observe the conditions that seem to be necessary for the development and growth of faith.

We cannot do the work of the Holy Spirit any more than a physician can do the work of healing, but we can be sensitive to the process by which growth and healing happen. When we become aware of conditions like readiness for abstract thinking, we can take advantage of opportunities to influence faith development.

At the very least, we can try to make sure that we do not hinder the Holy Spirit as God reveals himself in love and care. We do become hindrances when we try to nurture faith in ways that are beyond the developmental capacities of those we teach, or when we fail to provide opportunities for growth when readiness is there.

Though knowledge of faith stages helps us in nurturing faith, the stages are not a value scale that determines the relative worth of individuals or groups. Any one of the stages may be appropriate for a particular person or group. Each way that a person responds in faith to the love of God is full of grace and power for faithful living.

That a person at Stage 5 of faith-knowing may have a broader and deeper grasp of God's nature and presence than a person at Stage 3 does not mean that he or she is more worthy of the grace that has been received or is more loved by God. St. Paul wrote to the Corinthians: "What have you that you did not receive? If then you received it, why do you boast as if it were not a gift?" (1 Corinthians 4:7).

Implications of life cycle passages

What are the faith issues that a person is likely to face and struggle with at a particular point in his or her life? This is the question life-cycle studies raise for anyone nurturing faith.

If you cannot identify the crucial question that a person is asking or ought to be asking at a particular period of life, then the resources of faith that you bring to the person may be inappropriate and inadequate. The possibility of a person's growth in faith is greater when the revelation of God's gracious presence speaks directly to the particular needs of that person at her or his stage of growth.

Let us consider once more the beginning of faith and assume, as we have in Chapter 4, that trust is the foundation of faith and faith's basis throughout life. If that is so, then we ought to be paying attention to how we encourage and discourage the development of trust in the earliest stages of life.

Trust that is foundational for faith is more caught than taught. Many parents have the mistaken notion that their children learn to trust God first of all through Bible stories about trust, but these stories can evoke a positive response only when children know through prior experience what it means to trust in a reassuring presence.

Take the example of a young child being put to bed. The child is tucked into bed. Prayers are said. The light is turned off. As Mom or Dad begin to leave the room, the plaintive cry comes, "I'm scared."

What's called for at a time like that is not knowledge but a reassuring presence. You can use logic and state that no stranger could possibly get to this room and that you will be within hearing distance. But none of this will be convincing if the fear is strong. In other words, nothing that you *say* will be able to take the place of your *presence*.

Few parents associate experiences like this with teaching their children faith, that is, trusting. They are more likely to think they are teaching their children faith when they read them a story from the Bible, especially if the story is *about* trust. But the story about trust is likely to make sense only if the child has experienced a trustworthy presence in time of need and has learned to trust through such experiences.

The assertion that trust is foundational for faith has implications for church school teachers as well as parents. It is important to attend to the presence or absence of trust in the classroom at all times. Seating children in a circle rather than in rows and sometimes sitting with them on the floor can help create a friendly relationship of trust. Keeping the class size between six and twelve facilitates communication and a relaxed style of teaching which makes it easier for children to trust each other and their teacher. Time spent alone in interest centers also may nurture in children a feeling that they are trusted.

None of these suggestions necessarily creates a trusting environment and trusting people. What works for one teacher may not work for another. But the principle is clear: Faith needs a trusting environment in order to grow, and the nurturing of faith requires teachers who are sensitive to the basic importance of trust.

The importance of trust

If trust is the foundation for faith, then trust is important to everything that is presented for Christian religious learning. An appropriate question to ask of every Bible story used in the nurturing of faith is "What is the promise of God in this story, and what makes that promise trustable in my life and in the lives of those whose faith I am trying to nourish?"

That question is appropriate, even if the lesson of the day is about laws and commands rather than promises, such as a lesson on the Ten Commandments or the Sermon on the Mount. The principle is that the gospel and its promises must precede and undergird the laws and their demands.

Children learn to obey God by faith in the same way that they learn to obey their parents willingly. Loving obedience is learned within a context of love and acceptance. "We love, because he [God] first loved us," wrote John (1 John 4:19).

It was after their deliverance from the bondage of slavery and on their way to the land of promise that Israel received the Ten Commandments on Mt. Sinai. It was after Jesus proclaimed the coming of the kingdom and demonstrated its arrival by his healing and forgiving and by accepting outcasts of society that he delivered the Sermon on the Mount. Law does not nurture faith, but it provides a structure for relationships that are rooted in care and trust.

The same principle is true in the teaching of Christian doctrine. Baptism, for example, is gospel. It promises that we are God's children and that our sins are forgiven. The principle that trust is foundational for faith suggests that being God's children precedes and undergirds forgiveness, not the reverse.

The promise of God's forgiveness is trustable because as his loved children we cannot do a wrong so great that our dear Father would cast us away from his presence. Although forgiveness of sins is at the heart of the gospel, its promise rings true only for those who already know themselves to be loved by God.

Midlife caring

Space will permit only one more comment on the implications of life-cycle theory for the nuture of faith. From that theory we learn that the capacity to care is not fully developed until midlife, even though it is taught already in early childhood. But to most people in middle adult years, caring becomes so important that they may not remember that they were not always caring persons.

Parents are often upset when their children seem uncaring in their relationships with other people, especially with those in their family. Parents may even accuse their children of lacking Christian faith and spirit. As a result, their children may act caring just to hold on to the love they desperately want from their parents and siblings, or the children may be plagued by doubts about their Christian identity.

Parents who realize that a young child does not naturally have the capacity to take the perspective of others—a maturity basic for the caring aspect of faith—will be more realistic and patient in what they expect of their children.

Implications of faith patterns

St. Paul recognized different levels of faith-thinking when he said to the Corinthians: "When I was a child, I spoke like a child, I thought like a child, I reasoned like a child; when I became a man, I gave up childish ways" (1 Corinthians 13:11). Fowler has identified stages or patterns of faith that enable us to chart the process to which St. Paul alluded. Let us now consider some implications of this theory for the nurturing of faith.

Faith is nurtured more effectively through the telling of stories than through the teaching of doctrines. But how the stories are heard and understood depends on the meaning-making capacity of the individual.

Chapter 4 indicated different ways in which the Bible story of Abraham and Isaac might be understood by individuals at different stages of faith-thinking. The purpose of that presentation is to show that people hear and understand the same story in different ways, depending upon their level of faith development.

If this is so, then teachers will be more effective in their nurture of faith when they listen closely to how the story they are presenting is being interpreted. Most of the time we assume that different people are going to get the same meaning from stories that we see.

But almost every Sunday school teacher has at least one anecdote that illustrates the surprising ways in which children make sense out of what they hear. "Harold be thy name" is what some youngster thought the word *hallowed* meant. Such remarks evoke more amusement than wonder.

A teacher must anticipate and look for differences in the way learners make meaning out of what is taught. One very simple method of doing this is to ask children (and adults too!) to repeat what is presented to them. Then listen carefully for the different understandings that emerge.

It's important that we do not at this point attempt to correct what appears to us to be obvious distortions in the learners' understandings of the story or presentation. Correcting them would be imposing on them our way of making meaning.

I am not espousing the popular notion that each person is entitled to his or her own viewpoint. But I am urging that the limits of a person's way of thinking within a particular stage of faith-development be respected. And we need to facilitate the efforts of each individual to use his or her faith capacities to the fullest extent possible. Therein lies the most hope of helping people to move from one stage of faith to another.

Crosstage static

The principle behind what has been said in the previous paragraphs is that familiarity with stages of faith-thinking can contribute to an effective communication of the gospel. Apart from such considerations one risks what has been called "crosstage static." This occurs when a person attempts to communicate his or her faith at one stage to someone at another stage.

An example of this counterproductive effort at helping others to grow in faith is the unexpected reaction to the college student who is eager to share a newfound understanding of faith with parents who are operating at a Stage 3 type of faith. Some parents reject both the viewpoint and the child. Some parents respond by making a Stage 4 transition themselves. Still others draw their children back to Stage 3.

Most of the time the bonds of mutual trust and loyalty between children and parents are secure enough to tolerate and often resolve the tensions that are an inevitable part of a crosstage static. But some awareness of stage differences is a distinct help in living with such tensions.

Stages are normal

A key assumption behind the principle we have been considering is that the process of emerging stages of faith is natural and normal. This means that maturation (also in faith) is part of God's plan of how we come to know him and his will and ways. These stages need to be respected and fully taken into account in our efforts at nurturing faith in others.

Not all would agree. There are well-intentioned persons who urge us not to expose children to certain stories or ideas about God because such exposure may result in distorted imagery and thinking. Such a warning would be appropriate if the way a child makes sense of things did not change radically over periods of time. However, what may be a distortion for an adult is not a distortion at all at another stage of faith.

There are other well-intentioned persons who would place arbitrary limits on the growth of faith. This happens most often at Stage 3. At this stage, faith is conventional, meaning that what one believes is determined mostly by what the constituted authorities say is true. Many people are never challenged to grow beyond that Stage 3 level of faith-thinking.

Honest doubting is a sign of readiness for a transition to Stage 4. Persons whose faith is being properly nourished can accept such doubting as part of their growing into a more mature and more secure faith. Such faith is more mature because of a more inclusive stage of faith, a faith that does not eliminate doubt in order to protect narrow and exclusive ways of thinking.

God certainly wants people to use their capacity to grow in faith. Both the capacity and the opportunity for growth vary from individual to individual. So we can expect people to be at different developmental stages in their faith. Those who have responsibility for nurturing the faith of others certainly ought to do all within their power to facilitate maturity, even when this means that the student may outdistance the teacher.

Faith beyond Stage 3

I have mentioned the transition from Stage 3 to 4 a number of times. Let us consider the implications of this transition for the nurturing of faith. The movement is from external authority (what the church believes) to internal authority (what I believe).

People at Stage 3 of faith-knowing look to external authority probably because of their need to be accepted by others. Such acceptance gained by meeting the expectations of others generally works until the young person leaves home and meets people whose values and beliefs are very different from those of the church.

Such encounters can lead to a high level of defensiveness or to the adoption of a set of values and beliefs that meet the approval of the new authorities. Neither response is an advance over Stage 3.

Growth in faith beyond Stage 3 calls for an environment in which the Stage 3 person is not only permitted but challenged to make a confession of faith that is truly his or her own, a faith based on personal judgment and internal conviction. The environment needed is not a wilderness in which a person is left to find his or her own way, but a faith community that facilitates self-chosen commitments to a set of values and beliefs that are shared by others.

At the church-related school where I teach, students are required to take three courses in theology. They also have access to a chapel program that places a strong emphasis on worship and pastoral care. The university is like any other good liberal arts college in its training of students in the use of analytical and critical skills. Such a setting is an ideal location for the movement from Stage 3 to Stage 4 of faith-knowing.

Those students who make a successful transition are more firmly rooted in the church's life and practice than they would have been if they had been encouraged to circumscribe their faith during these crucial growing years. But the transition does not happen without considerable pain to some, especially those who are made to feel disloyal and unfaithful by well-intentioned authorities.

I have spent many an hour with students who experience a dark night of the soul in their struggle of faith. But the result is usually a stronger faith and a greater readiness to meet the challenges of faith that are inevitable in the post-graduation years.

So important is the nurturing of faith during stage transitions that the following section has been devoted to this concern.

Transitions and the nurture of faith

Both of the developmental theories presented in this book, life cycle and passages and patterns of faith-thinking, use the idea of stages and transition between stages. The word *stage* has been used more frequently than the term *transition*. The human life cycle has been described as unfolding stages, with development seen as a movement from one stage to another. Faith-thinking has been described in a sequence of structural stages, each more comprehensive and flexible than the previous one.

This emphasis on stages has been misleading if it has suggested to the reader a smooth and predictable movement from stage to stage. The journey of faith is full of trauma and crises, with crucial turning points that call for decision.

Erikson uses the term *crisis* to describe the conflict that must be resolved at the end of each stage in order to have successful transition to the next stage. Crisis is the term also used to describe the midlife transition about which so much has been written recently. The precariousness of a person's faith journey and the magnitude of the forces that threaten it are evident most clearly in the transitions.

Nature of transitions

What's involved in a transition? First, note that there is an ending. Most people ignore endings in transitions. All their attention is focused on the challenges of the next stage, the next job, the next marriage.

In teaching on a college campus I am a witness each year to the transition that every graduating senior must experience. I've sat through many a commencement address, but I've never heard one that even mentioned endings, much less used them as a theme. Nevertheless, for college graduates there are many painful endings of treasured relationships—a parting with friends who shared many intimacies, with mentors who modeled a life of faith and hope, with a community within which an identity was shaped.

Second, transitions carry people into a wilderness period, a time when nothing is quite firmly in place and the pervasive feeling is a sense of being at a loss. We're not who we were and not who we will be, and we are not even quite sure who we are. Though this is a normal and necessary part of a transition, it is unsettling, especially when there are not culturally established rituals to facilitate the movement between what was and what will be.

A third point worth noting is that transitions lead to new beginnings. Things fall into place, and the way into the future becomes clear. That does not happen all at once, and more often than not the new beginning is something that happens *to* a person rather than something the person chooses.

Awareness of the new beginning may come as we wake up one morning and realize that there is more order than chaos, more power to act than feelings of helplessness, more acceptance of self and world than self-doubt and self-contempt. As this happens, a surge of energy readies us for the new opportunities that make each new period of life and each new stage of faith exciting and challenging.

A stage transition is a painfully dislocating process of letting go and rebuilding. It means the dissolution of a way of being and knowing that was fairly stable and comfortable. It means living with ambiguity and a sense of uncertainty, often for a considerable period of time. It's no wonder that there is so much resistance to stage transitions, even when present modes of being and thinking prove constrictive and stunting.

The sternest tests of faith come in periods of transition. Israel was fairly comfortable in Egypt, even though they were slaves. Later they found their ease in Zion as they became settled in the land of promise. It was the journey through the wilderness that was their sternest test of faith. Complaining to Moses and doubting the providence of their God Yahweh, they yearned to escape from their freedom and return to the bondage of Egypt. So it is often with us and our students in the journey of faith.

Coping with the crises

In the periods of crisis there is often a need to go back to the roots of faith, back to trust in the promises of God and the hope that rests on such promises. When chaos threatens and we feel powerless to cope with forces beyond our control, when we expect to be judged because of our failures, when we feel impoverished because there is so little to nourish our sense of self-worth and competence, then we feel very small and fragile even as children of God. Especially at such times, we need what we have always needed from the very beginning—an awareness that we are being supported by a God who loves and cares for us and whose Son died for us.

The supreme example of trust sustaining faith through a period of transition is Jesus on the cross. All other transitions pale by comparison. For Jesus the crucifixion was a transition from death to life eternal; for the people of God it was a transition from Israel to the church; for the whole world it was a transition from an old creation dark with sin to a new creation washed clean by the blood of Christ.

Fully aware that the cross was the crisis point in the coming of the kingdom of God, Jesus felt the awful pain of dislocation and abandonment in that wilderness experience. He was forsaken by almost all who had supported his mission, which now seemed a total failure. Small wonder that Jesus felt forsaken even by God.

Nevertheless—and in this "nevertheless" is the trust of faith—Jesus called out, "My God, my God." It was trust that sustained him in the midst of chaos, loss of meaning, powerlessness, and a death that threatened darkness for all the earth. It was trust that nothing could separate him from the love of God.

It is such trust that we need to nourish in the stage transitions. Such nourishment comes from the Bread of Life that Christians receive through the Word of the gospel and the sacraments. Trust, nourished within the context of a total ministry of the gospel (through preaching, teaching, worship, Holy Communion, pastoral care, Christian fellowship, sharing of faith, and living the Christian vocation), will sustain Christians in season (periods of relative stability) and out of season (periods of transition).

Within a ministry of the gospel we need significant rituals at normal transition points. Fortunately the church is blessed with a number of such rituals, like Confirmation and marriage. But such rituals need to be examined in the light of what is known about transition periods, especially the dark side of those events: endings and wilderness wandering.

A Christian also needs rituals for nurturing faith through transition periods, particularly the midlife crisis and retirement, when greater support is needed.

Faith nurture in transitions

Following are some examples of faith-nurture in periods of transition.

One of the most difficult transitions children must make comes when they first enter school, especially if they have not had day-care experience. What is ending is a rather secure life in a home where parents or parental substitutes can be counted on to meet most of the needs of the young child.

In the home where the preschool child is rarely more than a loud shout from an adult, the world seems safe. Leaving that safe world is like a journey into a wilderness and can be very traumatic. Every new environment outside the home, including the church school, is part of a transition.

How can faith be nurtured effectively through this difficult period? First, the transition itself must be recognized —the ending of a total embedment in the home, the uncertain groping for a secure place in a strange environment, the beginning of a new challenge in a new world.

Second, pilgrim stories can be told, like the story of Abraham, the story of Israel's exodus from Egypt, the story of Ruth, and countless others in the church's biblical heritage. It is not necessary to make any direct application to the children other than to invite them to share their stories and their fantasies about trips to new and strange places.

Third, children need to learn about the God who promises to be with them whenever they go. They need to know that they are not alone and will never be abandoned as they take giant steps toward personal independence. God's loving, caring presence provides the most solid assurance that there is continuity between endings and beginnings.

Transitions common to adults

Transitions are as common to adults as they are to children, and for this reason their faith needs nurturing as well. A form of faith nurture that holds great promise for midlife transition is spiritual direction.

New forms of spiritual direction, which has a long history in Roman Catholicism, are being inaugurated outside as well as inside the church. By using techniques of meditation and journal writing, persons look deeply within themselves and listen closely to their inner spirit.

Adults at midlife hunger for such experiences. No longer occupied so totally by demands of family and vocations, they are ready to spend time exploring the meaning and value of their lives.

The transition into late adulthood calls for a nurturing of faith that links past and present, beginnings and endings. As life approaches its end, the past often seems more important than the future.

Older adults spend a lot of time telling stories of long ago, often the same ones to the same people, a habit which taxes the patience of those who share their lives. But they need to tell their stories, stories which sustain their identity and sense of self-worth.

Others also need to hear these stories, stories of a history now fading but rich in memories of promise and fulfillment—both divine and human. Perhaps through their stories we can recover the image of wisdom in the elderly who surround us. This will serve our own enrichment as well as the inspiration of children and youth.

A format for the telling of stories has been developed by James Fowler. Called "The Unfolding Tapestry of My Life," It guides one to reflect, throughout life, on places, relationships, marker events, authorities, images of God, and world events.[13] The advantage of such an instrument is that it lends both depth and scope to the telling of one's life story and thus adds to its value for both teller and hearer.

The relationship aspect of faith

Faith is relational to its very core. Beginning when God calls a person into relationship with him through Baptism, Christian faith is sustained throughout life through Word and Sacrament. Both are relational events through which God speaks to us and feeds us. Faith sustains us in the isolation of our dying because through faith we are related to a God who promises us that nothing can separate us from his love in Christ Jesus.

The assumption that faith is relational runs like a thread throughout this study. Erikson's theory of the human life cycle is often called a psychosocial theory, meaning that the individual is always living and growing in relation to a social context. Fowler's theory of faith stages is interactional, which means that everything we think and know is a product of our interaction with our environment, including our ultimate hopes.

Our brief review of the meaning of faith in both the Old and New Testaments reveals how deeply relational faith is, especially in the emphasis on faith as trust in the covenant promises of God. And nowhere is the relational character of faith more clear than in the earliest period of its formation.

In its beginnings faith is best described as trust, and trust remains the foundation of faith throughout life. We learn the meaning of trust and promise through the experience of relationship long before we have the language capacity to formulate such meaning. Language and meaning are an important part of our faith, but the life of faith is to be found in experience, especially the experience of relationships.

Parents can be the voice, the arms, and the breast of God in the loving of their children. In learning to trust the presence and promises of their parents, children learn to trust the presence and promises of God as mediated by their parents.

Not only in its beginning, but throughout the human life cycle, faith is relational. Identity is formed in community, both the identity that is "given" to and the identity that is "owned" by the young as they confirm those who confirm them.

Those who confirm the young have developed in mid-life the capacity for caring, a term that has no meaning apart from a deep attachment to the one cared for. Surrendering one's hold on secure anchors of identity in late adulthood is possible only for those who are sure that they are held securely by a God who will not let them go.

Relationship in the nurturing of faith

Because faith is so deeply relational in its nature, it is not surprising that the nurturing of faith also needs to be deeply relational. It is within a nurturing community that faith is most likely to grow and mature.

Persons, regardless of age, who are living and growing as Christians need support from a Christian community. They need experiences appropriate to the particular phase of their development. They need guidance in their periods of transition, encouragement and assistance in making crucial choices, and repeated assurance of the presence of Christ their Savior.

Congregations that are sensitive to the relational and developmental dimensions of faith will want to be nurturing communities through all of their ministries. It is my prayer that this little book will further such ministries. Faith is and will remain a mystery, and our clumsy theories and halting words cannot begin to deal with its nurture adequately. But pray God for the wit and will to try, and praise God for the growth in faith that often comes in the trying.

REFERENCE NOTES

1. For my understanding of scriptural views of faith, I will be drawing heavily on Hans-Jürgen Hermission and Eduard Lohse, *Faith*, Biblical Encounter Series, trans. Douglas Stott (Nashville: Abingdon Press, 1981).

2. Daniel J. Levinson et al., *The Seasons of a Man's Life* (New York: Ballantine Books, 1978).

3. Based on Erik Erikson's "Eight Ages of Man" in *Childhood and Society*, 2nd ed. rev. (New York: W. W. Norton and Co., 1964), pp. 247–274.

4. The most recent and readable presentation of this theory is to be found in James W. Fowler's *Stages of Faith: The Psychology of Human Development and the Quest for Meaning* (San Francisco: Harper & Row, 1981).

5. Theodore G. Tappert, ed. and trans., "The Large Catechism," *The Book of Concord* (Philadelphia: Fortress Press, 1959), p. 365.

6. Ibid., "Apology of the Augsburg Confession," p. 213.

7. Walter A. Hansen, ed., *Luther's Works*, vol. 4, *Lectures on Genesis Chapters 21–25* (St. Louis: Concordia Publishing House, 1964), p. 117.

8. Ibid., p. 119.

9. Ibid., p. 116.

10. Levinson et. al., *The Seasons of a Man's Life*, pp. 90–93.

11. Frederick A. Niedner, Jr., "Vocation as the Situation for Moral Discernment," *Promises and Faith: Readings for Introduction to Christian Theology*, ed. David G. Truemper (Valparaiso, Ind.: Valparaiso University, 1981), p. 100.

12. Frederick Buechner, *Wishful Thinking: A Theological ABC* (New York: Harper & Row, 1973), p. 15.

13. This instrument is in the process of being tested and refined by Fowler and his staff. Inquiries about its availability can be directed to the Center for Faith Development, Candler School of Theology, Emory University, Atlanta, GA 30322.